Anonymous

Indian Idylls

by an idle Exile

Anonymous

Indian Idylls
by an idle Exile

ISBN/EAN: 9783743357211

Manufactured in Europe, USA, Canada, Australia, Japa

Cover: Foto ©ninafisch / pixelio.de

Manufactured and distributed by brebook publishing software (www.brebook.com)

Anonymous

Indian Idylls

INDIAN IDYLLS

BY

AN IDLE EXILE.

CALCUTTA:
THACKER SPINK & CO.
1890.

CARPENTIER

PRINTED BY THACKER, SPINK AND CO., CALCUTTA.

CONTENTS.

	PAGE
THE MAHARAJAH'S GUEST	1
THE MAJOR'S MESS CLOTHES	7
IN A HAUNTED GROVE	19
HOW WE GOT RID OF HUNKS	32
MY WEDDING DAY	45
MRS. CARAMEL'S BOW-WOW	68
THE TABLES TURNED	79
A POLO SMASH	87
AFTER THE WILY BOAR	96
IN THE RAJAH'S PALACE	105
TWO STRINGS	119
A MODERN LOCHINVAR	128
MY FIRST SNIPE	142
MRS. DIMPLE'S VICTIM	151
LIZZIE; A SHIPWRECK	160
HOW THE CONVALESCENT DEPOT KILLED A TIGER	170
FAITHFUL UNTO DEATH	178
THE HAUNTED BUNGALOW	206
CHRISTMAS WITH THE CRIMSON CUIRASSIERS	220
IN DEATH THEY WERE NOT DIVIDED	238

THE MAHARAJAH'S GUEST.

PROBABLY as perfect a specimen of what a paternal Indian Government can produce, in the way of an anglicised native nobleman, was to be found in His Highness the Maharajah of Pugreepoor. He had been under the thumb of English tutors ever since his infant steps toddled out of the precincts of the zenana, and had been brought up on British ideas. As a result, at the age of five-and-twenty, he was a dapper little fellow, dark-eyed and Italian-looking, able to hold his own at cricket and polo against an Englishman, and as yet a stranger to the snares of the brandy bottle and the *nautch* girl, which had ruined, first the figures and then the brains, of so many of his ancestors, long before they had reached his age.

Pugreepoor was the husband of one wife, a dusky little nonentity, whose form, as yet "unfettered by stays," and whose feet, as yet "unspoilt by a shoe," he was having squeezed into the fashions of Paris, as reproduced on the banks of the Hooghly. Moreover, the impecunious widow of a general officer had been specially retained to teach the Maharanee deportment and manners, and to pioneer her through the intricacies of Anglo-Indian social etiquette.

For the Maharajah was gradually becoming one of the ornaments of society in Calcutta and Simla. He owned large tracts of land somewhere or other in the

Peninsula, and his income rivalled that of the richest of English dukes. He could command vast battues of tiger and big game in wide stretches of jungle, and equip with an army of coolies and elephants, globe-trotters of high degree, who were anxious to see something of sport during their scamper through India. But all the same Pugreepoor was not a reigning prince, and was only entitled to a very meagre salute of big guns at a durbar compared with many a bloated native potentate who could not write his own name, or read it either.

But Pugreepoor recked little of these things. He aspired to be English among Englishmen, and was already planning a visit to England during the Jubilee festivities. As London society takes very kindly to anything dusky, be it Red Indian or Hindoo, when once out of its own habitat, Pugreepoor hoped to spread his pinions and widen his horizons in the very highest spheres.

In spite of the rather negative attractions of his dusky bride, to whom he had been married at the tender age of ten, there was one lesson, taught by the customs of Anglo-Indian society, which Pugreepoor showed himself only too apt to learn—this was the noble art of flirtation. As a rule, a lovely woman in India has a holy horror of the native, however much her sisters in Belgravia may adulate him; for she knows but too well the point of view from which he regards her and her manners and customs. But gradually for Pugreepoor an exception was made. He was really not a bad-looking little fellow. He waltzed charmingly, and his wealth was so enormous that he was lavish with presents on the very least pretext where he was anxious to please. Slowly, but surely, the giddy gunner, the cavalier cavalry-man, the rising competition-wallah, some day to be worth his weight in pension, indeed even the fascinating A.-D.-C., with the sweet sisterly confidential manner to women, found himself distanced by the little Maharajah.

Little Mrs. Campbell, quite the prettiest woman up at Simla that year, who, in bygone days of happy memory, might even have had a poet-viceroy at her feet, threw over her last new pet A.-D.-C. and the young lordling in the Lancers, for Pugreepoor. Her taste may not have been unimpeachable, but his diamonds were irresistible. Nothing was now wanting to complete the Maharajah's English education. He was taken up as Mrs. Campbell's authorised " bow-wow," was taught to fetch and carry, and to stand patiently against the wall when not dancing with her, and worship from afar. For her was the pick of his stable; she sanctioned his guests to tennis and dinner, allowed him to go nowhere where she was not invited, and took him out calling, and even to church. Really, the Church Missionary Society owed her something for her praiseworthy efforts to reclaim this brand from the burning. Mrs. Campbell trained the Maharajah so well that she was even able to "lend" him occasionally to one or other of her female chums, to dance or ride with. This, be it observed, is the crucial test of a "bow-wow's" devotion.

Now, naturally enough, Mrs. Campbell, having taken all these pains with Pugreepoor, during the gay six months of a Simla season, was not going to let him escape again into the giddy whirl of Calcutta, while she returned to the dusty little station where Captain Campbell had been left to grill alone.

"Maharajah," she began in her most winning manner, as the pair cantered, after the races in the bosky vale of Annan, up the winding paths among the rhododendrons to the Mall, while the tree-crickets whirred overhead among the ilexes, and the coolies panted up under their fair burdens. "Maharajah, I've never been down to Calcutta. It would be real nice of you to ask me down for the race week. I shall just die at Dustypoor."

To speak was to be obeyed. The devoted Pugreepoor instantly made all the needful plans, and Mrs. Campbell selected his house-party for the races.

Even the happiest times must have an end. Government offices closed, the soldier's leave season came to an end, and there was a general exodus from the mountain Capua, and a ceaseless stream of *tongas* galloped down the road to the plains. The Simla world dispersed over the length and breadth of the Peninsula. But Pugreepoor went straight down to Calcutta, with the supreme Government folk, and began to install himself in his new bungalow in Park-street. Mrs. Campbell, meantime, meandered about some large stations, paying visits, riding at single anchor, as it were, awaiting the Maharajah's telegram to bid her fly south.

The Calcutta trades-people had a fine time of it, and rejoiced exceedingly that Pugreepoor was going to do the thing in style this year. When everything was ready he dispatched the brief wire to Huddelabad, which was to gladden Mrs. Campbell's heart—

"All ready. Come at once."

But to his intense surprise he received an answer which staggered him for a moment—

"My terms are three hundred rupees a month and all found."

But Pugreepoor was too much *épris* to hesitate. Evidently the golden-haired one was in a playful mood. So he telegraphed forthwith—

"Terms be hanged! Come at once!" And knew no peace till he received an answer to say that Mrs. Campbell would arrive by the evening mail, which came in in time for dinner.

So the Maharajah set to work and collected a little party *in time* to dine with her on arrival. There was first and foremost the people's Bill (that is to say, the people's Bill in India—no connection with a personage bearing that *sobriquet* in England). There was that rising young secretary Ben Blewett, and his charming wife, one of the three lovely sisters known throughout India as "Faith, Hope, and Charity" (Mrs. Blewett was Charity, because her kindness to mankind was so universal that it covered a multitude of sins). With her came, as a matter of course, the high official to whom Blewett was indebted for his rapid promotion. Then there was the most popular Adjutant-General that ever breathed, beaming and boyish; young Lord Scamperly, the A.-D.-C.; and, last but not least, Mr. Justice Squirrel, of the High Court, with several brand-new stories.

The train was late; it often is, when it steams into Howrah station after its three days' journey from Peshawur. Everyone was assembled in the palatial drawing-room awaiting Mrs. Campbell's arrival. Amid the roar that followed one of Mr. Squirrel's stories (given as a sherry-and-bitters just to stimulate people's appetites for something better to follow) even the Maharajah's expectant ears failed to hear the carriage drive up.

The heavy *portière* was flung back, and a rustling white-robed attendant announced—

" Mrs Campbell!"

An unwieldy old woman, whose *métier* was but too plainly indicated by her appearance, waddled into the room, and panted out to the petrified Maharajah—

" How is the lady, sir? I 'opes I'm in time!"

Poor Pugreepoor! In his haste he had forgotten that there might be more than one Mrs. Campbell in a large place like Huddelabad.

THE MAJOR'S MESS CLOTHES.
A True Story.

IN Major Munnie, Paymaster of the Royal Scilly Islanders, was to be seen one of those few remaining specimens of Crimean officers still to be found floating about the subordinate ranks of the British army. His contemporaries, the men with whom he had scaled the heights of the Alma or shivered in the trenches before Sebastopol, had mostly gone up higher, in every sense of the word. But lack of gold, in the days of purchase, had kept poor Munnie from rising; and now for years he had been seated, metaphorically, in our pay office, the lawful object whereupon the impecunious subaltern might vent alternately his powers of importuning and wheedling. He was a shrunk, dapper little man. His little remaining hair had run to seed in floating grey whiskers, such as Leech's warriors wear in old *Punches*, at the period when only " plungers " went in for what they termed "moustachios." He was a good old boy, and we of the Scilly Islanders all loved him; and in converse proportion, we all loathed Mrs. M., his better half. And his better half she was in more than one sense, though not in all. To begin with, she would have made about two and a half of the little major; and secondly, even to the most casual observer, it was apparent that she had indeed bettered her position in life when she married him, though who she was and how it had come to pass was a secret, for ever locked in Munnie's bosom. Mrs. Munnie exhibited a tendency to cultivate upon her upper lip the hirsute appendage which his ancient traditions forbade to the major. She was also, in her domestic way, quite as great a financier as her husband.

Report said that the poor little major, who all day long dabbled his fingers in the coin of the realm, never had an anna he could call his own, but that madame doled him out such as she thought good for him, and kept a stern eye on his mess bill. He had all our sympathies, especially towards the end of the month, when pay day was approaching and we wanted him to let us overdraw. We would be profuse then in our invitations to come and dine with one or other of us at mess, and in other small ways try to give the poor old boy a little fun on the sly.

At the time when this veracious history took place the Scilly Islanders had just been moved to a capital station, which I will call Guramghur. The Munnies took up their abode in a corner bungalow, facing the barracks, and Ruffleby and I chummed in the next corner bungalow. Between us and the Munnies, back to back, as it were, with the latter, and so facing our bungalow, resided a black-and-tan family of the name of Hooper. Hooper *père*, who wrote the magic and elastic initials P. W. D. after his name, was thin as a lath. Madame, on the contrary, after the manner of Eurasian women of middle age, presented the appearance of a feather-bed tied round the middle with a bit of string. Their two daughters, however, were

THE MAJOR'S MESS CLOTHES. 9

only whitey-brown, and as pretty a pair of little girls as you could wish to see. Ruffleby and I soon became acquainted with our neighbours, for they lived a good deal in the verandah, where madame was constantly to be seen in an appalling state of *déshabille*, rowing her servants from the depths of a huge armchair. In the cool dusk of the evening Ruffleby and I, riding down the Mall, would walk our ponies by the side of the little " Hoo-poos," as we had christened them, who tripped daintily down the watered roadway in patent-leather shoes and white stockings.

On Sunday, the Hoopers, along with the rest of the dubious-complexioned population of Guramghur, occupied seats in the gallery of the station church. It was an old-fashioned Georgian edifice, probably built in the time of the first Afghan war, and with a melancholy association to all who studied the graves in the whitewalled cemetery close by. All the European garrison of Guramghur were at church parade that fateful Sunday in May 1857, when the mutiny broke out in the native lines across the canal, and were minus their arms. The rebels seized the latter, shooting down their officers, and decamped for Delhi, leaving the European troops defenceless and powerless. Since then, in Guramghur as well as all over India, the British troops take their rifles to church with them and lodge them in sockets in the seat in front.

But to return to our Hoo-poos. We subs, who herded together in a seat behind our superior officers, soon established a system of signals and telegraphic messages with the fair ones in the gallery, which somewhat militated, I fear, against the benefit we should have derived from the chaplain's discourses, especially when in addition MacQuinsie, our funny man, would make his own interpolations.

Soon after our arrival at Guramghur, our sergeants gave a dance in barracks, to which, of course, they invited the mess, on a card of leviathan proportions. Having ascertained that the little Hoo-poos were to be among the guests, we laid ourselves out for a lark, and invited some equally festive spirits among the gunners to come and dine and go with us.

As Ruffleby and I went out for our evening ride, we passed on the Mall the Munnies' barouche and seedy pair of grey countrybreds. Mrs. M. was taking the major out for his drive. The poor old boy looked dreadfully bored.

"Look here," I said to Ruffleby, "let's ask the Backsheesh Sahib to dine, and take him with us to-night. He looks as if he was very down on his luck."

"Happy thought," rejoined my companion; "I must get a hundred rupees advance out of him next week, or I shall be on my beam ends, so it'll be as well to get him in a good temper."

"We'll tell him he'll meet the little Hoo-poos. I'm sure he's rather smitten in that quarter, for I've noticed he always sits and smokes in his back verandah now, so that he can look over into their compound and watch the fair young things at play. But, by Jove, Mrs. M.'ll never let him come!"

"Leave it to me, I'll square her," cried Ruffleby, and he cantered after the carriage.

"Have you met the colonel, major?" he cried. "He wants to see you particularly; was asking where you were just now, when I left the mess."

Unsuspecting, Mrs. Munnie had the heads of the greys turned messwards, and Ruffleby joined me hastily.

"Once in the mess, I'll keep him safe. You ride back to his house, and tell his servant to send his mess clothes over to the mess at once. He must dress there. Quick! Before the old girl gets home!"

Our plan succeeded admirably, for the prisoner was only too willing to be caught. The bearer and the clothes arrived, and with the assistance of a stiff peg the major was emboldened to send a note back by him, to the effect that he was going to dine at mess.

We had a very festive dinner. The paymaster's hilarity almost equalled that of our guests, and he became a different man. Ruffleby whispered to me he should ask for two hundred at least.

Dinner over, we adjourned to the sergeants' mess in little companies of twos and threes. Some drove, some rode their own or other fellows' ponies, some tried to walk, and at least three mounted on Derehurst's old grey Arab, commonly called The Omnibus, because he was in the habit of conveying two or three fellows to mess.

The sergeants' mess was a bower of beauty, tastefully decorated with evergreens and pink-paper roses. The gallant non-coms were deep in the seemingly endless mysteries of the Circassian Circle when we arrived. This was succeeded by the Triumph and Payne's First. Out of consideration, perhaps, for every-one's toes, round dances were in the minority. Between the dances there was no sitting out in dark corners, such as was wont to obtain at some dances which we Scilly Islanders have given. The warriors, in stiff tunics buttoned up to their throats, promenaded round and round the room with their partners, or conducted them to the peg-table, and gave them hot sherry.

"And now, Mrs. Maacartney, an' what'll ye take?"

"Thank ye, kindly, I won't take anything. I had a thurst, but I've quinched it."

Into this paradise of decorum, inhabited by fair creatures with divers-coloured necks and gorgeous frocks of aniline hues, we, the new arrived, imported, I am sorry to say, an element of rowdyism. We introduced each other all round, to such fair ones as attracted our individual attentions, under high sounding names, and the promotion was most rapid in the Scilly Islanders that night.

I had just finished, notwithstanding the scowls of a leviathan bombardier, in presenting " Lord " Derehurst to a pretty little woman in a red dress, the exact shade of her red arms and neck, when I felt my elbow nudged. The pay-master jerked his head towards the little Hoo-poos.

"Introduce me to our fair neighbours, my boy."

I steered him across the room to the vicinity indicated. Why will Eurasians always dress in white? They looked very pretty, all the same, preening and bridling, with orange bows in their dark hair, for all the world like the cheeky little crested Hoo-poos who infested the verandah. They were twittering in their soft *chee-chee* tongue to a circle of admirers who made way for us.

"Miss Hooper, allow me—introduce Major-General Munnie, C.B.—Aide-de-Camp to the Queen (whisper)—who—most anxious—make your acquaintance."

"Oh, my! You don't say! Noa? I never did one real general know, at all!" And the dark eyes were fixed reverentially on Munnie's bald head.

Here my colour-sergeant collared me and led me off to drink more hot sherry, after which the regimental sergeant-major and the pay sergeant repeated the process. I have no very clear or exact recollection of the events of the ball. The temperature of the room was a hundred and something, and the betunicked sergeants shone and trickled and mopped, and then shone and trickled and mopped again. The floor was very heavy for dancing, and very hard for falling. I was charged in a wild polka by a Hussar sergeant about six feet two and ignominiously floored. I have a vision of old Munnie standing up in Sir Roger about 2 a.m. (the dance had begun at eight sharp) with one of the Hoo-poos, whom he tried to kiss as he turned her round. Imagine Mrs. M.'s feelings had she seen! I could not exactly say what time we most of us got back, somehow, to our own mess for some grilled bones. Ruffleby and I escorted the pay-master thither.

"In for a penny, in for a pound, you know, major.

Must have some supper. None waiting for you at home, you know!"

The vision of what was awaiting him at home, poor old boy, was so appalling, that his spirits only revived again after supper and champagne. Then, somehow or other—one never knows how these things begin—there was a good deal of promiscuous bear-fighting, and a slaughter of the ante-room chairs and settees. I know I had one lamp-shade, two tumblers, and a pane of glass down in my next mess bill. The couches and chairs we shared equally. I also had a bruise on my left shin, which nobody paid me for.

While Ruffleby was dancing a fling down the mess table (the marks are there on the mahogany to this day) some of us trussed old Munnie and the doctor with billiard cues, and set them to cock-fight. It was the event of the evening. I backed the pay-master, and lost my money. A wild chorus of the last new comic song was going on round the piano, to which Derehurst was giving a brandy-and-soda, because he declared it was out of tune, and wanted picking up, when some of us had to lend a hand to pack our guests the gunners into one of the *tikka gharys,* or flies, which had been parked out patiently in the compound all night. We laid Ruffleby on the roof full length, as we could not make him sit up anyhow, and he eventually got to his bed I believe. Then I found old Munnie at my elbow again, very dejected.

"Look here, my dear boy, what ever am I—do. Daren't go home like shish—shink of the missus?"

He indeed presented a pitiable sight. There was a huge knick in his trousers, besides rents where there had once been brace buttons, one sleeve of his mess jacket was torn out, the shoulder straps were wrenched off, and it was split up the back, the result of his trussing. What was to be done indeed!

"You won't leave me, my dear boy; see me through it, there's good fellar."

I swore never to desert him, and we wended our way somewhat disconsolately down the road in the light of the glorious Indian full moon.

"She mustn't shee 'em. Never let me dine at mess again. What shall I do? Sure to find them to-morrow. Always looks into all my drawers," moaned poor Munnie, as we approached his residence.

"She *shan't* find them, major," I said; "we'll hide them, and you can telegraph to Calcutta for some more. She must not find them at any price."

"No go, my dear fellar; always looks everywhere. Keeps my keys, you know."

We were standing actually in the gateway. In another minute we should rouse the slumbering *chokedar*, and see the dreaded vision of Mrs. Munnie prepared to welcome us in the verandah. Suddenly an inspiration seized me. I dragged the pay-master into the shadow of a tree and tore off the remains of his mess jacket.

"Quick, major!" I exclaimed in a whisper hoarse with the awful gravity of the situation. "Quick! Slip off your trousers. Cold be hanged! We *must* get rid of them. We'll bury them here in this flower-bed."

Two Eugene Arams engaged in concealing some hideous deed of darkness could not have worked with greater alacrity and trepidation than we two did there in the shadow of the mango tree. Happily the ground was soft, having been just dug and irrigated by the *mallee*, and in a very short space of time the last vestige of scarlet and gold lay concealed beneath the surface, and we breathed freely.

The shivering major skipped, in his airy attire, out into the moonlight and up the steps. He was nearly knocked down in the verandah by a rug hurled at him from behind a half-opened door, and a voice thundered—

"Take that on to the drawing-room sofa. For it's all you'll get this morning."

When I ran against Munnie coming out of his office next day, his face lit up with a smile and a wink as he flourished a telegram at me.

"All serene. The new ones'll be sent up in a week. I'm saved!"

Ruffleby got his advance without a word of demur, and the sky seemed clear.

Not quite, though. We had a misunderstanding with our little Hoo-poos, which led to their transferring their fickle affections to two fellows in the artillery. It came about on this wise.

My stable-companion and I had arranged, the one an early morning walk, and the other an early morning ride with our fair neighbours. At 6 a.m. Hoo-poo number one, tired of waiting, for her tryst with me was

THE MAJOR'S MESS CLOTHES.

for 5-30 a.m., sent over to my bearer to awake me by force.

Knowing, by experience, how utterly futile is any attempt to din a European name into a native's head, she merely told him to rouse the little sahib. There is a matter of a few inches between Ruffleby's height and mine. But the valet was more than usually crass.

He awoke the wrong man, and, after a lapse of twenty minutes, returned to Miss Hooper with hands clasped, and a *désolé* expression.

"Missy sahib, your honour, protector of the poor. I have done my best. Four times have I got the sahib out of bed—once, even, have I got one leg into his trousers—but he always turns into bed again, and says he is not the man!"

My Hoo-poo declined to accept this explanation. A coolness ensued with the above-mentioned result. A few days later as I left barracks, the adjutant asked me to follow the pay-master over to his bungalow and mention to him some official matter which had escaped him.

I found Munnie and his lady seated in the verandah, the former refreshing himself after his arduous duties with an ante-tiffin peg. Madame received me grimly, I thought, so I hastened to broach the subject of my visit.

I was interrupted by the bearer's appearance with the daily post, and a brown paper parcel came by parcels post. Munnie looked at me and seemed embarrassed. Mrs. M. regarded him sternly.

"What have you got there, Munnie? Open it at once, and let me see what extravagance you've been up to now?"

The pay-master obediently but nervously cut the string. I wished myself anywhere else.

"It's only a new suit of mess clothes, my dear," he faltered; "mine were getting rather shabby," and the neatly folded garments fell on the matting before him.

Mrs. Munnie rose to her full height and advanced glaring at him, repeating in tones of thunder, "Rather shabby, are they?" and she disappeared into the house.

I looked at Munnie, Munnie looked at me.

"Don't go, my dear boy—you're not going!" implored my accomplice, seeing me glance round as if to escape.

At that moment the *mem-sahib* reappeared suddenly. Her expression was enough to quail the stoutest heart, and she brandished aloft before our conscience-stricken faces the exhumed mess clothes, muddy and tattered.

"Rather shabby, are they?" she repeated. "I should rather think they are!"

I was a base coward, for—I turned and bolted. Ever afterwards the poor old Backsheesh Sahib was never allowed to dine at mess, except on Christmas and other rare occasions, when we had a ladies' dinner party, and he could be accompanied by Mrs. M.

IN A HAUNTED GROVE.

THE following is a little episode out of the days when my husband, an officer in the Engineers, was in civil employ in India, and held the appointment of superintendent of what I will call the Guramghur and Ganges Canal. Now the life of a canal engineer is slightly monotonous. It may be a degree higher in social status to that of an engineer in charge of one of the State Railways, and it may embrace a wider sphere of action than that of engineer in charge of barracks or fortifications in a garrison station, but it lacks variety. During the cold weather, for six months on end, we marched up and down that wretched stream, which ran through as uninteresting a tract of country as is to be found in Northern India. At each halting-place—and I got to know them by heart, as they were placed at regular intervals of ten miles or so along the bank—the same pitching up the same camp, with everything in each tent exactly the same as it had been the day before. Outside, the same muddy, sluggish stream, with its painfully regular banks, planted with the same tamarisk, acacia, and such like light trees. We marched in the early morning, arriving at our new abode by breakfast-time, and found the mess-tent pitched, and the patient cook preparing our repast in the open air over a grate scooped out in the sun-baked earth. After breakfast my husband held a kind of little court. The headmen of the neighbouring villages appeared.

Always the same mutual grumbles between them and the sahib—too much water le tout over their rice-fields, or not water enough; arrears of dues to be paid; and an everlasting finding fault with the native subordinates in charge of this portion of the canal, corrupt and untrustworthy as all native officials are, and who, as usual, had pocketed the money and neglected to keep up the banks. A slip and a flood were quite an excitement in our life.

Such an event had occurred at the time of which I am writing. The heavy showers that generally fall in Northern India about Christmas-time had come earlier than usual, and we found our habitual camping-place under water, and our tents pitched for us in a square grove of mangrove trees, about half a mile from the canal, and within a few hundred yards of a native village of mud huts. It was not at all a bad place—shady, which was a consideration at noon, even at that season of the year—and a change from our usual surroundings. So we decided that it would do very well for us to halt in for Christmas Day.

Christmas Day is kept by the English in India, however remote and lonely they may be, and in spite of utterly uncongenial weather and surroundings, in a way that has much of pathos in it. There is a melancholy striving to keep Christmas as "at home"—a going to church where possible, gathering together of friends and acquaintances, a decorating of church and gateways with flowers, and much feasting—all which hollow mockery does not still the longings for home, and the thoughts which will fly back to days that are no more.

Our Christmas on the canal was generally lonely enough; but, on this occasion, we were looking forward with delight to the advent of two visitors. One was our old friend, Colonel Rydale, an ally of many years' standing, now retiring and going home for good, and who had promised to come and spend Christmas with us on his way down country.

The other was Jack Denver, a subaltern of artillery, quite new to India, and new to us also, though we were very anxious to make his acquaintance; for Jack had just come out from England, engaged to my youngest sister Lily, who was to follow and marry him a year later.

Our younger guest arrived in camp first, riding across country on a new purchase, ahead of his coolies and luggage. The colonel came later in our dog-cart, which we had sent to meet him at a point where the canal was crossed by the high road, and which brought him thence along the canal bank, a road strewn with ugly holes and pitfalls for the unwary.

"Now, Bob," I said to my husband before dinner, "listen to me. You'll have plenty of Colonel Rydale who is not pressed for time; but Jack must go on to his battery the day after Christmas Day, and I want to find out what he's like; so, after dinner, you go and have a quiet smoke with him alone, and I'll entertain the colonel. Men always wax confidential over a pipe. I like the look of him well enough, but I don't believe he's half good enough for dear Lily."

Bob did as he was bid (he always does), and, after dinner, I found myself sitting in the dining-tent alone with my elder guest, while Bob carried off Jack to smoke in the office tent.

It was a lovely moonlight night, such a night as you only get in the tropics, but chilly withal, for the wind was rising, as if rain were coming. We had a little charcoal fire in our portable stove in the tent.

Colonel Rydale talked of many things and people over his coffee, but at last I got him on to the subject nearest my heart.

"Colonel Rydale," I asked, "do give me your opinion about our young friend yonder; I am so interested in him for my sister's sake."

"Seems a nice fellow," the colonel replied, "what I've seen of him. Well-set-up and smart, and no nonsense about him. Odd thing, you know, but he reminds me so in appearance of a great chum of mine I lost when I was a young fellow and quartered at Punkahpore in this district, not far from here."

"Indeed," said I; "and was he nice, your friend?"

"A better fellow never breathed; and good-looking too—just the image of that boy."

"Poor fellow! And what did he die of?"

"Die? He didn't die; that's the funny part of it. Queer story altogether. I never could make it out—he was lost—missing—not heard of."

My feminine curiosity was roused.

"What a strange thing! Do tell me, Colonel Rydale."

I poured him out another cup of coffee; I bade the bearer bring him a live piece of charcoal wherewith to light a fresh cigar, and, thus encouraged, the colonel told his tale, what there was of it.

"It's many years ago; I was a youngster, so was Jack—his name was Jack, too. We did everything together; shared the same bungalow, rode together, shot together. One of our favourite haunts for snipe was a *jheel* (morass) near this very place. We often came out here, and I recollect it because Jack admired very much a really very handsome native girl, whom we saw drawing water at the well near the village over there. We laughed at Jack in the mess about her, and the headman of the village, one of whose wives she was, got jealous, I think, and shut her up and would not let her show herself when any of the sahibs came this way shooting. She really was a very pretty girl—so tall and slim and graceful; an oval face—and such eyes; not a bit like the average native woman."

"Well, colonel," I laughed, "she seems to have made an impression on you too, after all these years, for your memory to be so fresh! But I am more interested in Jack."

"Well, it was one Christmas. I was ordered away suddenly on detachment duty. Jack took ten days' leave, and went shooting. It was a splendid snipe season, and there were lots of black buck in this part then. Well, Jack went away on leave two or three days before Christmas. The day after Christmas his bearer, the only servant he had with him, turned up sick with fever, saying his master, who was at an old rest-bungalow not far from here, had sent him back because he was so ill. Well, do you know, Jack was never seen or heard of again. The district was scoured, the natives all interrogated, and there came a rumour that he had taken a dâk-gharry (a post-chaise) and gone down the Grand Trunk Road towards Calcutta. But it was never confirmed, and no trace of him was ever found. The civil officials did their best, but Jack had utterly disappeared. His name appeared in orders, after a bit, as absent without leave. After a month or two it was struck out of the service in the official Gazette."

"But was there no reason for his disappearance?" I asked.

"None that I could ever find, except that the poor fellow was very hard up, and owed a lot of money. But that was the case with several of us in the 'Dashing Drabs' in those days. A court of inquiry sat on his affairs, and we raised a subscription among us, and paid up, that the name of the old corps mightn't suffer, and also because we all missed poor Jack so. No, it was a rum affair altogether. I didn't understand it at all, and I never shall."

At this moment the entry of my husband and Jack cut short our conversation, and soon afterwards I retired to my tent, leaving the gentlemen to sit up a little longer over their pegs.

My tent had been pitched a little way from the others, in a corner of the square, regularly-planted grove, under a particularly fine mango. I got into my dressing-gown, dismissed my ayah, and, anxious to lose no time, sat down to begin at once a letter to Lily for the next mail, with an account of my first impressions of Jack Denver. I was busy writing when Bob came in and went to bed, and to sleep promptly, for he had had a worrying day in office.

Presently I finished, and putting away my letter—so eulogistic and so sanguine—raised the curtain of the tent door, to have a whiff of air before getting into bed.

The brilliant full moon, sailing at intervals from under scudding clouds, flooded the wide-stretching level plain with a haze of silver, and cast inky black shadows in the grove under the mangoes. But for the rising wind the night was very still. Now and then a bark of a *pariah* dog echoed from the neighbouring village, or the distant yell of a jackal. But there was a silence in the night, a silence which might be felt. I stepped outside to enjoy the peace and beauty of the scene, and, as I did so, the weird hoot of a startled owl among the branches made me turn my head towards the grove.

Then I perceived two figures advancing towards me out of the deep shadow—two—a man and a woman.

They came nearer out into a patch of moonlight, and I gave a gasp of surprise as I recognised them; for the man was Jack, my Lily's Jack, and he was walking with a native woman.

I stepped back against the tent and watched eagerly, much shocked; for she was a very beautiful woman I could see now the moonlight was so strong—graceful and lissom in her scanty drapery, and—oh, horror!—Jack had his arm round her waist, and her head was leaning on his shoulder.

I dropped the curtain of the tent, and stood within thunderstruck at what I had seen. Of course, I had heard rumours in India of Europeans taking unto themselves the daughters of the heathen; but that Lily's Jack, so young, so new to the country, should pursue such a course so openly, and under my very nose, shocked me almost as much as if it had been Bob himself. What faithlessness! what profligacy! My poor Lily!

There lay the letter in which I had been praising up to the skies this precious young scamp. What a mercy it was that I had not sent it—that there was yet time to warn her as to the real character of the man whom she contemplated marrying! I tore up the letter I had written, and, with a strange whirl of anger, surprise, and distress in my mind, flung myself into bed, and soon fell into a troubled sleep.

How long I had slept I do not know, but I was awoke suddenly by the whining of the little terrier Nip, who always slept at my feet. Nip was standing bolt upright in bed, with his ears back, his tail between his legs, and his attitude cowering. He was gazing intently at the door of the tent, and whining in a queer frightened manner. My first thought was of thieves, and I sat up promptly and looked in the same direction.

A second or two later, though the curtains did not part, I distinctly saw two figures pass through them— one like Jack in English clothes, the other a draped native female, whom he clasped to him.

They advanced slowly across the tent, and I sat and glared at them. Suddenly, as they came nearer, my heart froze within me, for I saw that they were headless.

With one shriek of terror I fell back senseless on to my pillow.

When I came to myself it was broad daylight, and I was lying on a long bamboo chair in the dining tent. As I opened my eyes, Bob bent over me, and a wonderful expression of relief crossed his face. I grasped his hand convulsively.

" Bob!" I cried, " for God's sake, don't leave me."

" I'm not going to, darling; but you must be quiet," and he laid a wet rag on my burning brow.

" But where am I ? Why am I not in bed—in my tent ? "

" There was a heavy storm in the night after—after you were taken ill. The gye ropes gave way and the gusts nearly blew the tent down, so I carried you in here. Are you feeling better ? "

As he spoke, the memory of the awful vision I had witnessed rose up again in all its appalling ghastliness, and I suppose I must have looked pretty bad again, for Bob forbade me to say another word. He put on fresh cold applications, and the ayah came and fanned me. Under these soothing influences my bewildered brain grew gradually soothed, and I slept.

It was a wretched Christmas Day after all, for all of us—we who had expected to be so jolly together. I dozed all day, afraid to think, not allowed to talk, dreading the night with a nameless horror. How thankful I was, then, towards evening to find myself being lifted into an extemporised doolie, and being borne away from that awful spot.

"Where are you taking me, Bob?" I asked feebly, for my head was getting bad again.

"On to the next camp, my darling. We think it will be better for you. You've got fever here."

I noticed, in a vague kind of way, there was a queer look in his face, very unlike his usual expression. He looked rather scared.

"My head's bad," I replied; "but I'm not very ill—don't be alarmed about me, Bob."

I meant to tell him what I had seen, but the horror of it again overpowered me, and I closed my eyes to shut out the ghastly sight.

Then the coolies came in and carried me off. I don't remember anything about the march or the new camp, for the morning brought on a sharp attack of fever, and for many days I lay unconscious and delirious. Colonel Rydale stayed on to companionise Bob, who was really anxious about me, and sent in forty miles for the nearest doctor.

I got better. My brain recovered its equilibrium, and I was able to think with less horror of what, but for Nip's extraordinary behaviour, I should have thought a bad dream.

One day I lay languidly in a long chair. We were to march on the next morning and resume our regular routine, and our guests were leaving us. They were sitting by me now, and I feebly watched the colonel light a cigar.

"What an odd ring that is on your little finger, colonel?"

He dropped the match as if he had been shot, burning a hole in his trousers, and muttering to himself for doing so.

"It's not native work, is it?"

"No, French," he answered shortly.

"Do let me see it."

Rather unwillingly he let me draw his hand down and examine it.

"I see, it's one of those French *porte-bonheur* rings, a twist of gold and silver. A keepsake, eh, colonel?" and I laughed nervously, for as I touched the ring a cold creepy feeling came over me, and those two awful figures seemed to float before my eyes again.

"A keepsake? Yes," he replied shortly, "it belonged to my friend Jack."

Here was an opportunity to disburden my mind of its awful secret. Mastering my horror with a violent effort, I sat up and spoke.

"Colonel Rydale," I said, "I have seen your friend Jack."

The colonel jumped up amazed.

"Good God!" he exclaimed.

"Yes," I went on, with increasing difficulty, for every word I spoke seemed to conjure up the vision afresh, "I have seen him twice—on Christmas Eve—in the mango grove—with a beautiful native woman. The first time I thought it was Jack Denver—the second time—in the tent—Nip woke me, howling—and I saw——"

I could not go on. I covered my face with my hand as if I could blot out the sight, and the colonel, very alarmed, mixed me some stiff brandy-and-water. Then he looked at me fixedly.

"Do you feel stronger? Can you bear to hear something?"

I nodded assent.

"We have found him—Jack—the next morning, Christmas Day. They were righting your tent, which had been blown down, and in digging a trench round to carry off the water they came upon——"

"Go on," I muttered.

"Two skeletons together—headless—the skulls detached—chopped off. On the wrist and ankle-bones of one were a native woman's bangles; on the little finger of the other this queer ring poor Jack used to wear. That's why we moved you off in such a hurry. Hullo! Here, Bob—come, quick—your wife has fainted!"

When I came to, I asked to see the ring again. It seemed to have a fascination for me, this link between the poor murdered lad of years ago and the present.

"I remember the ring well," said Colonel Rydale. "We used to chaff Jack about wearing it, and he always persisted in saying it had been given him by a sister, who was dead."

"There's something engraved on the inside," I remarked, twisting the ring round and reading aloud, "J—a—c—k, f—r—o—m L—i—l—y—B—a—r—n—e—s."

Jack Denver, who had not spoken hitherto, now jumped up with a start.

"Good Heavens!" he exclaimed, "show it to me! That was my mother's name before she married. Yes, I knew she had a brother who died in India, but after her death I never saw much of her family, and I have never heard any particulars. What a round world it is, to be sure! That poor fellow must have been my uncle!"

Instantly the resemblance between Jack and that figure I had seen, flashed into my mind, and as quickly explained itself satisfactorily.

Lily and her Jack were married within the year, and are as happy as the day is long, but I have never had the courage to breathe to her my suspicions of her lover on that awful night.

HOW WE GOT RID OF HUNKS.

THE moral of the following tale is most reprehensible, and the only excuse I can offer for relating it is the lame one, that it happened a long while ago.

We youngsters of the Royal Scilly Islanders were a wild lot rather in those days. But our wildness chiefly arose out of the intense happiness we all felt in serving together in that distinguished corps, which we fondly believed was equalled by none in the service. Not a very humble opinion, to say the least, but one which I still hold as strongly as ever.

I have called ourselves the Scilly Islanders, because I have no wish that the reader should penetrate the disguise of this veracious history, or set about speculating forthwith as to whether we wore bonnets or bearskins, rifle green, or British scarlet. Suffice it that we bore the names of a score of glorious victories on our colours. But we were by no means a wealthy lot of fellows, or with special fame in racing, cricket, &c. (Polo in those days was played only by the natives on the Assam frontier, and had not penetrated to England, or even reached India.) No, our great distinction was that we were the Islanders, and that was enough. Promotion was slow, for gold (it was in the days of purchase) would not tempt fellows to leave, and as for the ranks, when short service was, as yet, an unknown thing, the men were born and died in the regiment.

HOW WE GOT RID OF HUNKS. 33

The epoch to which I am alluding being, of course, before the blissful dawn of the Cardwellian competitive examination era, you could only get into the Scilly Islanders by way of a nomination from an Exalted Personage, who was honoured by being our Colonel. How it was, therefore, that Hunks managed to get gazetted to us we marvelled greatly. We came to the conclusion that the paternal Hunks, whose name to this day you see on reels of cotton, but fail perhaps to recognize as Lord de Hunsby (the de Hunsbys came in with the Conqueror, he has found out), had lent the Exalted Personage money.

In any case Hunks's appearance followed that of his name in the gazette, and he burst upon our astonished eyes when we were quartered at Punkahpore. He arrived, attended by many native servants, who were plundering him freely, and brought kit enough for a married man with a family, including an English dog-cart, and three Arabs he had bought at Bombay for four figures (in rupees) each, and who all presently turned out unsound. He arrived, and, before dinner was half over the first night at mess, he had put our dear old Commanding Officer's back up by enlightening him as to how things were done in his, Hunks's, elder brother's corps, the Green Dragoons.

"As if the Scilly Islanders wasn't a pattern to a dozen of your d——d swaggering heavies," the old man muttered fiercely over his night-cap " peg " later on.

Then he dilated, and with a calm assurance which was exasperating in the extreme to our Major, the

C., M. G. 3

younger son of one of the most historic commoner families in England, on the glories of the *famille* Hunks. He related how they had bought up a fine old estate in Wessex, and built a palace on the site of the old hall; and how they rented half a Scotch county from several heads of clans too poor to live on their properties. The Major looked him down from head to foot, but writhed visibly in his chair. By the time the wine was on the table he had informed another of us that his mamma, whose pet and darling he appeared to be, intended him, after he had seen a little soldiering, to marry a well-known beauty, the dowerless daughter of a pauper peer of high degree.

"And I don't think she'll do badly, by George!" quoth Hunks, complacently, filling up his glass with our best champagne (with which he found fault), in blissful ignorance of the fact that the Lady Grace to whom he alluded was first cousin of the man sitting opposite him. But the mess president was down upon him like a shot, and informed him that ladies were never mentioned by name at the mess of the Scilly Islanders.

But trying to set down Hunks was like trying to squash an india-rubber ball; his rebounding power was wonderful. (We had christened him Buggins, by-the-bye, as soon as we heard him announce that his name was Marmaduke Algernon de Tracy Hunks.) Nevertheless, we all made very fair attempts to succeed in our laudable endeavour. The hot weather was just coming on, and life was a trifle flat at Punkahpore, so Hunks-baiting became the fashionable diversion amongst us youngsters. Poor fellow! what a life we led him! Any thinner skinned person must have suffered tortures, but his armour of conceit was impenetrable. Nothing could pierce *that*. But we suffered too. The mere contact with Hunks made us feel such miserable paupers, even such of us as were not "deep in the banks." Little Ruffleby and Dick Derehurst who lived opposite the lordly bungalow where Hunks had taken up his abode in solitary grandeur, said they could smell his money across the road. Fancy a brass bedstead and English furniture upholstered in chintz, for a newly-joined subaltern, when a camp bedstead in the middle of a white-washed room, surrounded by bullock-trunks, was enough furniture for any of us!

Before many days were over the fiat went forth amongst us that Buggins was to be suppressed, or we of the Scilly Islanders would know the reason why. The seniors winked at our little games, loathing the newly-joined one as much as we did. We had nimble wits amongst us, and were of an inventive turn of mind. It was Derehurst and Ruffleby who packed up Hunks's entire kit one day when he was at recruits' drill, and littered his room with his own cards, with "P.P.C." written on them in the corner. I strongly suspect that the Captain, who was Lady Grace's cousin, had a hand in covering Hunks's magnificent gilt mirror with big cards, bearing fictitious invitations to Marmaduke Algernon de Tracy Buggins, from the Grand Lama of Thibet and the Governor-General downwards.

Someone else labelled the contents of his splendid morocco photograph-album with every big name in the peerage, and each night nearly we drank champagne at Hunks's expense, by fining him a magnum for breaches of regimental etiquette, into which we laid traps to lead him.

One evening a few of us detained him late in the billiard-room where he was being initiated into pool, while a band of others stole round to Buggins' Castle, as we had painted the name on his gate. When our hero at length sought his couch, what was his horror to find his washerman's donkey securely tied down in the English brass bedstead, making the apartment uninhabitable for the night, much to the delight of the spectators concealed in the verandah, awaiting the *denouement*. We took him out shooting, and afforded him the pleasure of shooting a village pig and a turkey-buzzard, and of bringing them home in triumph as a wild boar and a wild turkey. After a diligent morning's walking in the sun after snipe, over a dried-up *jheel*, where there would be no long-bills again for some months, he succeeded, when nearly exhausted, in killing a hoo-poo. This he ate for lunch, to the delight of the entire mess, including the mess-sergeant and the waiters, as his first snipe. We sent him solemnly in state, in his dog-cart, to call on the wife of the most influential native of the place, who caught Hunks on the threshold of the *zenana*, and would have thrashed him if he dared. We put a stuffed cobra into his bed, and slipped a dead whipsnake down the back of his collar after mess. But all was of no avail. Hunks appeared to find himself very comfortable with the Scilly Islanders. The fellow was not only a cad but a fool, and did not seem to know when he was being bullied.

The rest of the garrison, smart gunners, dashing hussars, began to chaff us about "Our Buggins," and to hint what an ornament he was to our corps. His latest *mots*, his most recent exploit, were retailed with a guffaw even over the mess table of the native infantry officers, whom we looked upon as not fit to black our shoes. We felt we were becoming the laughing-stock of the station, that some of our glory was departing from us, and all on account of Hunks!

Things had reached this pass when Captain Smylie, one of the smartest men of the regiment, returned to duty after a long spell as aide-de-camp at Calcutta to a Governor-General who was now going home. We were always very proud of Smylie. In every way he had been quite the neatest thing produced in the way of aides-de-camp for some years, and we youngsters especially thought a great deal of Smylie's opinion about anything.

It was a great shock for poor Smylie when he returned to the old corps to find Hunks rooted in it as if he had joined years ago. I can see Smylie now, the first night at dinner, his eyeglass fixed in his eye, and his quietest, most urbane manner on, carefully dissecting Hunks, and the latter absolutely giving himself away. Little Ruffleby tumbled off his chair with laughing.

"We can't—a—keep that—a—boy," remarked Smyli to a select few, late in the evening. "He must be returned: not up to—a—sample."

We all assured our mentor we had done our utmost to rid us of him.

"He's a wart on the face of the regiment," Smylie went on.

"My dear fellow," put in Derehurst, "you've not the remotest notion what we've suffered from him. Only the other day I overheard one of the black regiment fellows speaking of us as 'Buggins' Own.'"

Smylie knocked the ashes off the end of his cigar with the air of a man who has made up his mind.

"This must be put an end to. He must go. *I'll* see to it."

Now we all felt that a man who has spent some years at an Indian viceregal court, grappling with the precedence code and the invitation list, and who knows to a T who ought to take down whom to dinner, and such-like weighty and momentous questions, was not likely to be at a loss how to deal with a Hunks; so we went to bed elated.

Smylie had brought back with him to the regiment the handsome Arab chargers whereon he had been wont to figure in gubernatorial processions, as well as two or three smart ponies which he had used as a means of locomotion on the mountain paths of Simla. One of these, Shaitan by name (an appellation which will not bear translation), was a perfect little fiend. In appearance reddish-brown, with white face, and rolling eye; he was fast and handy, and altogether delightful when you were once on him. But in his stable no one but his groom dare go within reach of his wicked hoofs or teeth, and as often as not he had to be blind-folded before Smylie could mount him. For the Shaitan was what is called a man-eater. If handsome is as handsome does, never did a pony's character so belie his looks.

It was one evening after mess; the night was dark but sultry, for the hot weather was coming on apace, and we lay in long chairs in the verandah smoking. Hunks, who was on duty that night, was holding forth about the price of something or other he possessed, I forget what, and Smylie was drawing him out.

Suddenly the striking of the hour by the sentry at the guard-room in barracks, on a piece of iron hung up for the purpose, and which did duty as clock, rang out into the still night air, and reminded our hero that it was time to go and take the guard.

"What a bore!" he exclaimed. "I forgot to tell my pony to come for me."

"Perhaps he forgot to tell your groom," remarked Smylie, dryly; adding, "I've a pony here, take that."

No one in India ever sets foot to ground if they can help it, and the guards were some quarter of a mile away, so Buggins accepted the offer.

Smylie shouted for the groom; there was a vicious squeal in the darkness, and we all knew he had proffered Hunks the Shaitan.

The darkness favoured Buggins in getting on the pony quietly, and, in blissful ignorance of the animal he was bestriding, he disappeared out of the compound. Smylie called back the groom who was for running behind him as is the custom.

"Don't you go with that 'Sahib.' Let him manage the pony himself."

We fell to talking again. There was a consumption of whisky and soda, and we awaited Hunks's return. Time passed. He might have taken half a dozen guards and have been back by now. What could have happened? Had he forgotten the password and been fired at, for in India the sentries were then loaded?

The trotting of a pony up the drive interrupted our conjectures. We all rose up and hailed Hunks.

No answer. The Shaitan trotted up to the steps of the verandah *alone*.

We cautiously retired, for there was an evil look in his eye. Smylie directed the groom to catch hold of his bridle. The pony seemed hot, as if he had been ridden hard. But where was his rider?

The groom bent over the little beast, and extracted with difficulty something he held between his teeth and was shaking savagely.

Smylie took it into the mess-room, and examined it in the light. It was a piece of a scarlet mess-jacket.

In mortal alarm lest the Shaitan should have made mincemeat of the unfortunate Buggins, we provided ourselves with a lantern, and set off in search of him. We had not proceeded far when we fell in with him trudging dejectedly along in the dust, holding his arm.

"My cap was brushed off by a branch of a tree. I got off to pick it up, and the brute came for me, neighing, squealing, biting, kicking. I ran for it and got behind a tree, and he's dodged me round it for the last half hour, and I think he's nabbed a bit out of my arm."

His crestfallen appearance, and the vision he conjured up of hide-and-seek with the Shaitan, was too much for most of us. But we found, on inspecting him, that the pony had left his mark on Hunks, and that the victory remained with the quadruped.

Next morning, when our hero opened his eyes, he was surprised to see the regimental doctor and Smylie standing by his bed.

"How do you feel this morning?" asked the former.

"O, very fit!" replied Hunks, "except my arm's a little stiff where that beast of a pony's teeth scratched me."

The solemnity deepened on the countenance of the other two, and they looked at each other.

"Do you feel at all thirsty?" asked the surgeon again.

"Not more than usual in the morning," said Hunks. "Last night was a dry night at mess."

"Any queer feeling in your throat?"

"What on earth are you driving at? No, my throat's all right. Yes—no—well, perhaps, a little——" (swallowing).

Another meaning look between Smylie and the surgeon. Hunks grew alarmed.

"What's up, doctor? Do tell me. Is there cholera about?"

He got quite white, for we had frightened him well about cholera.

"O, if it was only cholera——," began Smylie.

"Hush!" interrupted the surgeon, warningly; "not a word. Nervousness might bring it on."

"For God's sake, doctor, have done with this and tell me what's the matter," cried poor Hunks, sitting up in bed in an agony.

"Tut! tut!" said the doctor, soothingly. "Calm yourself. Drink a little water."

Hunks pushed the proffered glass away in a rage.

"D—— the beastly water! I insist on an answer. What's the matter with me? *Will* you tell me?"

Smylie looked at the doctor. The doctor looked at Smylie, and then both looked from the glass of water to Hunks, and shook their heads solemnly.

"I implore you!" beseeched the victim. "I can bear the worst."

"Shall I?" asked Smylie of the doctor.

"Well, perhaps there is no use concealing it *now*," replied the latter glancing at the water.

"Well, then, my poor fellow," Smylie went on, "I grieve to have to tell you that the Shaitan who bit you last night has developed this morning serious symptoms resembling hydro——"

"Oh! not hydrophobia," gasped Hunks. "It's dogs have it, not horses."

"In this country, alas! horses too," corrected the surgeon. "His behaviour last night was very odd."

"Indeed it was!" gasped Hunks, clutching his arm. "Oh! my poor mamma! What will she say? Doctor," he added, seizing Jones's hand imploringly, "what can you do? Is there nothing you can recommend. Save me, I implore you! My people will make your fortune if you do."

Jones shook his head. "I have so little experience in a case like this. Your symptoms are serious: your throat you feel, your dislike of water——"

"If I were only at home within reach of good advice," Hunks cried in an agony. "Doctor, can't you get me sent home at once?"

"Your only chance, I should say," replied Jones, as grave as a judge. "If it could be managed——"

"It must; it shall be managed," Hunks continued hysterically. "I must be off overland immediately. Smylie, there's a good fellow, I implore you go and see the Colonel for me."

"I think I can manage it with a sick certificate," said Jones. "Your case is urgent."

And it was managed. The next steamer removed Hunks from India's coral strand, and from the Scilly Islanders, never to return. The shock had been too much for him and his mamma, who never let him out of her sight again.

I do not know if he ever gave Lady Grace the honour of refusing him ; but I know, when I saw her last, it was at a ball the Scilly Islanders gave to the Exalted Personage when she was her cousin's wife.

Shaitan was alive and kicking for many years after Hunks bolted home, but his temper did not improve with age.

MY WEDDING DAY.

I AM left alone, for the first time in my life. It is my birthday too. I am nineteen to-day. I had almost forgotten it with no one near to recall it.

Quite alone, save for the tiny pink blossom of a baby dozing in the arms of the ayah in the next room. By-the-bye, he has a birthday to-day, too. He is five weeks old; a little fragile hot weather baby, yet how much he is to me already, and with what a pang I surrendered him to the aforesaid ayah!

Alone at a hotel in an Indian hill-station! Roger brought me up here, and then had to return and grill in the plains. Poor Roger! But he has gone through so much hot weather. I could grill no longer, and they ordered me away as soon as I could move.

Oh! the terrible heat! What a blurred recollection of suffering and stagnation are the last few months since the furnace life began. It makes me shudder to look back upon it.

Up here the air is like champagne, and life seems once more worth living. But my reflection in the glass shows me still a very white little face. Ah! what a colour I used to have at home!

Home! How lonely the very word makes me feel. What a long way off home seems! I never felt lonely at home. How could I when there were eight of us, all in a small country vicarage. How I miss them all! I should like to show baby to the girls.

I miss Roger, too. I've such a sense of safety when he is with me, just as I have with father, and we have never been separated before.

Roger will miss me a little, I think. He is gone back to sit in that stifling court-house from six in the morning till twelve. Then when he returns to a late breakfast, I shall not be there to pour out his tea. Afterwards, he will go to sleep till it grows cool, when he will drive down to the racket-court, just as he has done for so many hot seasons before he married. But he will not miss me as I miss him. I can't go back to my old life.

We have been married nearly eleven months. Yet, somehow, Roger always seems to me just as he did when I first saw him. Good and kind he always is; but so much older, so far wiser, so far removed from me. Even at home they never thought me the clever one among the girls. How inferior I must be to Roger then!

It is just a year since we met. He had run home on three months' privilege leave, thin and tanned.

The first Sunday that he was stopping at the Hall, and sat in the Hall pew, I remember he looked at me all church time, and how uncomfortable he made me feel. Then, after church, Harry asked father who the "old fossil" was. They had no idea what a great man he is out here, a little King ruling a district as big as an English county!

I've sometimes asked Roger what made him single me out of all the girls. I am not so tall as Lucy, nor anything like so clever as Kate.

But Roger would never answer. He would only smile, and try and stroke my hair smooth.

Dear mother! I shall never forget how her eyes filled with tears when I came up to her room that night when Roger had asked me to marry him (after the tennis party at the Hall), to tell her all about it, and ask her what I should do.

How fervently she kissed me. "Indeed, Lily, you are a lucky girl! He's a good man, and then an Indian civilian is always worth three hundred a year, dead or alive!"

Three weeks later we were married, and the next week I left them all for India.

I remember I did not think much of mother's words at the time, but when I came out here to the big house, the tribe of servants, the horses, and the carriages, it was all very nice. If only the others could have seen and had a share in all my grandeur! We were so poor. It seemed almost wrong for me, little Lily, to go driving about in a big carriage and pair, while poor, tired mother was tramping about the village at home.

Oh! how doubly lonely and heart-sick it makes me to write and think about them all. I feel so utterly forlorn. Even Roger gone, Roger, who a little while ago seemed almost a stranger.

As I write, the great Indian full moon streams in at the open window, with the never-ceasing chirping of the crickets, or the distant baying of a pariah-dog. The moon is sailing away placidly in a cloudless sapphire sky, above the dusky forest-clad precipices, and over the deep, dark, silent lake. But even she is altered. She can't be the same pale, tremulous moon that used to peep into my little room at home!

And I am altered, too. It is impossible that I can be the same Lily she used to find there.

What a noise of laughing and talking. It will wake baby. It is the company dispersing from the *table d'hôte*. I have had a little dinner alone here. I shall never summon up courage to face that long tableful of smart women and military-looking men, all by myself. It was quite enough of an ordeal when Roger was here to protect me. I am always shy with strangers, and never did the talking at home.

There! A weak little whine like a kitten's. They *did* wake baby. I must go to him.

*   *   *   *

Since I wrote the above I have been dining out all by myself! How very brave of me! And my courage has been rewarded by having a very pleasant evening.

It came about in this wise.

Mrs. Carruthers is the wife of the Commissioner here. I don't exactly understand what a commissioner is. At home I know he's something unpleasant, something to do with taxes. Here, I believe, it is the next step above Roger, who often talks of the time when he will be a Commissioner.

Anyhow, Mrs. Carruthers is a great lady, and rules society. I feel rather afraid of her. The Carruthers are old friends of Roger's, and he introduced them to me one day when we met them on the Mall, as I was being carried along in my "dandy." My dandy! How I sometimes long for the boys to see me, when I go forth for my evening walk, borne aloft like Guy Fawkes on men's shoulders in an armchair. Wouldn't they laugh!

Mrs. Carruthers was very affable. In answer to Roger's apologies she graciously consented to forgive my not having called, and hoped I would come and dine quietly one evening when I was stronger, and left alone.

I did not dare to get out of the invitation when it came. Besides, Mrs. Carruthers seemed motherly, and called me "dear."

The room was quite full when I went in. I wondered what the Carruthers called dining "quietly." And I had on only a little white muslin frock.

In my character of bride I was taken in by Mr. Carruthers. I shall be thankful when I have been married a year, and have done with all the dull old gentlemen at dinner.

Happily, Mr. Carruthers seemed too hungry for conversation. He eats no lunch, after this dreadful Anglo-Indian fashion, and is consequently starved and irritable by eight o'clock. So he just introduced me to my neighbour and settled down to gobble up his soup.

Captain Tressinger, a tall man, rather bronzed, with a long fair moustache and a pair of bright blue eyes, bowed, and looked down at me.

I don't remember much about the dinner, though I am always trying to remember other people's *menus*.

I don't remember any of Mr. Carruthers' remarks, all interspersed with Hindoostanee expressions, which he had to explain.

I don't even remember much of what Captain Tressinger said. I fancied he did not talk much, only looked a great deal. Anyhow, presently I found myself chattering away as if I had known him for years. At home they always said I was a chatterbox when I was not shy. And he looked at me so kindly.

After dinner (how sorry I was when Mrs. Carruthers nodded at me as the signal to rise) there was music. Mr. Carruthers had indigestion, I presume, for he went to sleep in a big chair, and almost snored.

The room was very hot, and I was still far from strong and felt weary with the unwonted excitement. My flushed face suddenly turned cold, and the room began going round. I hastily made an excuse to get out into the verandah for a gasp of fresh air. Once out, I flung myself into the nearest chair, and closed my eyes, feeling as if I should faint.

Suddenly, some one bent over me. It was my neighbour at dinner, asking if he should call Mrs. Carruthers, or get me anything.

I implored him not to make any fuss, only to leave me alone, and closed my eyes again.

But he did not go away. He took my fan and began fanning me gently. In a few minutes I felt much better, and said I would go back to the drawingroom. But Captain Tressinger would not let me, and sat down in a chair by my side.

It was a lovely night. The bright moon lit up the depths of the lake below, and the mountains all around. I felt too tired for much talking, and lying back in the chair, enjoyed the stillness and the balmy night air.

Inside some one sang a song about the "Fairies." The refrain—"And you shall touch with your finger tips the ivory gates and the golden," came through the open window to us, and passed on into the still night.

Suddenly Captain Tressinger asked, looking down at me,

"Do you believe in fairyland?"

I smiled, and answered that of course no grown-up person does. Then I sighed, and added, that I used to fervently, and wished I could now.

He looked at me a little, curiously, as, somehow, I never remember having seen anyone look before.

"I do!" he said in a low voice.

"What *do* you mean?" I laughed, at the idea of a big man like that believing in fairies.

Then he explained.

Somewhere or other he had read that once, and once only in our lives, some one leads us to the ivory gates and the golden, and puts the key into our hands. Once, and once only do the gates open for us, and we catch a glimpse of fairyland. Sooner or later, all get their glimpse; some get a short one, some a long one. But all get a deep one once in their lives. To some it comes early, to some late; to some *too* late, he added sadly.

There was a silence.

I did not quite understand what he meant. I suppose he noticed it, for he added :

"You have not had your peep yet, I feel sure. But some day you will, and then remember what I told you, will you?"

Just then there was a stir within. Some of the guests were departing, and I rose and went in to take leave too.

I was packed up in my "dandy" and started homewards. I had not gone very far when there was a clatter of ponies' hoofs behind me down the path, and Captain Tressinger came up and asked if he might see me home.

I was still nervous over my "jampannees," lest in the dark they should stumble in these rocky paths and drop me, and I was only too glad not to be alone, the moon cast such inky shadows under the trees.

By-the-bye, Captain Tressinger talked a good deal about the moon as he walked home by the side of my "dandy." He quoted poetry. I am rather afraid some of it was Byron. Now, at home, we girls were never allowed to read Byron. But it was very pretty.

I am interrupted in writing this by a caller. The servant brings in the card.

It is Captain Tressinger. I'm *so* glad.

* * * * *

I am ashamed to find my poor diary has been dropped again. What will Lucy say? She made me promise when I went away I would keep a diary.

It dropped in the hot weather when I was so ill. But, when I came up to the hills and was left quite alone with baby, I took it up again. I seemed to need some one to talk to.

But lately I've not been nearly so much alone, for I have found a friend whom I can talk to as much as I like.

This is Captain Tressinger, and our friendship dates from Mrs. Carruthers' dinner party.

He is the first *real* soldier I have ever known. When he's on duty he appears in uniform. And very well he looks in it. (If I were a man I should always wear my uniform.)

He is living in this hotel, and, thanks to him, I have summoned up courage to face the *table d'hôte* meals again. The tepid food brought me in my own sitting-room was not nice. Captain Tressinger sits next to me, and I don't feel shy. All the other gentlemen are very civil and kind.

This is a strange new life I am leading up in this lovely nook in the Himalayas. I am beginning to feel quite strong, the air is so cool and keen.

It is indeed a lovely spot. The lake lies in a cup, like the crater of an extinct volcano. All around rise steep, wooded precipices covered with ilex and cypress and rhododendron, with here and there a red blossom left, for in April they dyed the mountain-side crimson.

The lake is green and deep, and sleeps placidly under the shadow of jutting crags on one side and of the willows on the other.

It is all more beautiful than anything I ever dreamt of. I said one day to Captain Tressinger that it was like fairyland.

He answered that it *was* fairyland to *him*. He is very kind. Nearly every day he comes and takes me for a walk. It is very dull to go out alone, carried aloft to the music of the "jampannees'" grunts and groans. So I am only too glad, with Guy Tressinger as a guide, to lose myself in these beautiful paths, winding in and out, among rocks and precipices, through ferny woods and by mountain sides, with far spreading views of plains and snows.

Sometimes in the afternoons, when it is hotter than usual, and we feel lazy, we go on the lake. We take the Canadian canoe and Guy paddles, while I loll on cushions at the other end. Then, where the shadows are deepest and coolest under Smuggler's Rock, we generally come to a standstill altogether, and Guy smokes, while I talk, or lie and watch the mysterious lights and shadows of evening floating over lake and peak. The prayer gong sounds from the Hindoo temple on the shore, vespers ring out from St. Mary's Convent in the trees, and a chorus of frogs comes up from the reeds by the water's edge.

One day Guy Tressinger did a fearful thing that almost makes me shudder to write about.

Far over our heads, on the precipitous cliffs, grew a rare fern. I, heedlessly, said how I wished I could get it.

Guy said nothing at the time, but after a while, when he had finished his cigar, he flung away the end, and paddling to shore, tied up the boat under a tree. Then, almost before I knew what he was about to do, clambered up the rocks, hanging on by his hands and toes.

I got dreadfully frightened; it looked so fearfully dangerous. A single false step might have sent him headlong, not into the lake, but to be dashed to pieces on the rocks below. I called to him as loud as I could to come back, that I did not want the fern. But he only turned his head with a smile and shouted back that it was all right.

Worse followed. He found he could not reach the wretched plant from below, but had to climb up above it, and then hanging down head and shoulders over the precipice, reach down to it with one hand. It was too horrible to see! I fairly screamed aloud and hid my face in my hands that I might not see him.

Presently, I don't know how soon, he was back again by my side, and touched me on the arm, holding out the ferns.

I suppose I looked up with a scared face, for he looked distressed.

"Did I really frighten you? Oh! I'm so sorry! It was nothing, you know."

"Promise me, promise me that you will never do anything so dangerous again. I can't bear to see you!"

He looked at me, for a moment, strangely, as if about to say something. Then suddenly he turned away sprang into the canoe and seized the paddle.

"It's getting late and damp for you to be out."

His voice sounded forced and husky.

Then without a word he paddled home fast and furiously. But when I got in I was surprised to find it was not really so very late after all.

* * * *

Ten days have passed since I wrote in my diary. Only ten days—and yet what a change they have brought!

All, all is altered! The veil is torn from my eyes, the illusion over. I see now the precipice that yawned at my feet.

No longer am I the light-hearted, innocent girl, but a woman, a hundred years older. A miserable, conscience-stricken woman.

Now I see plainly how Guy Tressinger loves me; and I—with shame let me confess it—I know that in my heart of hearts I love him as I never dreamed I could love anyone.

With him I am happy. Without him, I am restless and wretched till he comes again. My life seems to hinge on him, to consist in his presence, in hearing his voice.

I look back to before I knew him. I see now how starved, and cold, and loveless my existence was. I look forward with despair to a future in which he cannot, may not, find a place.

All this I feel to be wrong—dreadfully, desperately wrong! But I can't help it.

It has overmastered me, overpowered me. I know it is love!

What have I done that I should be so happy and yet so miserable; that I should taste this bitter-sweet—this pleasurable pain?

For the last few weeks I have been living in a fool's paradise. It *was* fairyland, the fairyland of which Guy spoke that evening when first we met. He has given me the key. He has opened for me "the ivory gates and the golden."

And this one short glimpse of fairyland has changed all the world to me. Who can come back from such a golden vision and view the commonplace earth with the same eyes again? Oh! why did I ever go in? And yet I hug to my heart the peep I have had!

This is how I awoke out of my dream.

There was a big ball at the Assembly Rooms by the lake, to which I was persuaded to go. The Carruthers said it was *the* ball of the season, and that I ought to go if only for once.

Then a great wish came over me for a dance and to wear a certain new ball-dress that had never even been unpacked.

Lastly, one day Guy begged me, with that strange, imploring look of his, which now, alas! I understand so well, to go to please him.

I had never in my life been but to one big ball, and that was the Hunt Ball. It had seemed to me gorgeous, inasmuch as the gentlemen wore pink. Imagine then, what I thought as I entered the Bachelors' Ball and found nearly all the male portion in uniform, including fat old Mr. Carruthers, in a nondescript coat with brass buttons they told me was something political.

In the gallery a scarlet and gold Lancer band discoursed soul-stirring waltzes. My dress was pretty; I felt young and strong. I knew I could dance; partners crowded round. At my elbow was Guy Tressinger begging for as many dances as I would give him, and then—oh, intoxicating bliss!—whirling me off in his arms into fairyland.

What wonder if I lost my head. I was only mortal, and it *was* fairyland.

Then came the awakening.

We, Guy and I, were sitting out in the dim verandah overlooking the lake. There was no moon, only stars. All was dark and mysterious. The sound of the music mingled with the night breeze in the trees and the lap of the water against the building.

They were playing "Mia Cara." Ah, me! those melancholy, deep low notes will haunt me to my dying day.

We had the corner all to ourselves, no one within earshot. I do not know how long we had been there. Guy had been talking rather hurriedly and excitedly. His face was close enough in the dark for me to see how flushed it was, how brightly his eyes shone, and how fiercely he tugged at his moustache.

There was a silence.

Even I, the chatterbox, was silent. I was with him. I was happy—too happy for words.

Something made me afraid to break the silence. I felt as if I were treading on a volcano which might burst under me at any moment. It was like a lull before a storm; as if the air were hot and stifling, the thunder rumbling, and in another moment the torrent of passionate words must fall.

I suppose an older, wiser woman than I, with more knowledge of the world, would have stopped him. But I was only a child, and unwittingly my heart was all his.

Then it came.

"Tell me, why were you so frightened the other day when I climbed up Smuggler's Rock?" He asked it earnestly, and his eyes asked it too.

"I frightened? Oh! I—I was afraid—it was very silly—afraid you would fall and be—hurt yourself." I could not say killed.

"Did you care? Would you have cared if I had?" he continued incoherently. His hand stole nearer mine, took my fan from me, and played with it nervously.

I looked up. I do not know what answer I meant to give. But I met his eyes. They seemed to burn me through, and I never answered anything. There was no need for words.

Then I let my head droop, my heart beating like a sledge hammer, so that I could scarcely breathe.

"I'm going away soon," he went on, after a pause, hurriedly and hoarsely. He bent down over me, his breath fanned my cheek.

"My time at the depôt will be up very soon, you know, very soon now. My peep into fairyland is over, our peep, may I say *our* peep?" He seized my hand.

"Lily, say you're sorry. Oh! say you'll miss me!"

I looked up and it was a moment before I grasped his meaning. Going away!

"No, no, I can't have you go!"

It broke from me unawares, and then, over-strung, I covered my face with my hands and burst into hysterical tears.

The grasp on my hand tightened till it hurt me. Just then the music ceased and couples of dancers came streaming into the verandah.

Guy rose, and leaning over the railing, stood there looking down into the dark lake.

I fancied I heard a groan.

Then a feeling of horror got possession of me. I felt afraid of myself, afraid of him, like a hunted creature brought to bay.

Mastering myself with a violent effort, I rose quickly and left the spot.

At the door of the brilliantly lighted ball-room, I found Mr. Carruthers, for a wonder, wide awake at this hour.

"I've got such a headache. Would you be so kind as to get my 'dandy' for me? I must go home."

Happily, Mr. Carruthers is very short-sighted. I felt thankful for it. It was but a short distance back to the hotel, but the maddening waltzes rang through my fevered brain all the way.

I went up to my room, and pulled aside the curtain that separated it from baby's. Then I let it fall again.

No! I felt I could not face that little innocent, with my guilty secret weighing on my soul.

I paced the room restlessly, full of conflicting doubts and fears and self-reproaches.

Then I took off my ball-dress, and pulled the flowers off my head and bosom.

Oh! that wretched ball; why did I ever go to it?

The room seemed to stifle me. I flung open the window and sat down at my writing table. The night breezes cooled my fevered head. Almost mechanically as it were, from the need of confessing to some one, I began to write my diary.

It has done me good. It has calmed me, though I feel as heart-sick, as despairing, as before.

A faint glow of dawn is perceptible in the air. A cawing of half awakened crows comes in at the window.

Another day has begun. The beginning of a life all changed for me. Suddenly with a start I recollect it is the anniversary of my wedding day.

* * * * *

I have come across the above sheets of an almost forgotten diary, kept years ago when I first came to India.

The chapter of my life to which they refer is closed for ever. The wounds are healed if the scars remain. So I will now finish the story of my wedding day.

Since then we have had many anniversaries of our wedding day, but none, thank God, like the first. Roger and I are staunch friends, if lovers we have never been, and have weathered together many blazing hot weathers and drenching monsoons.

Our children are growing up around us. The little white cross, underneath which sleeps my little lost darling among the everlasting hills, was all moss-grown and ancient-looking when last I visited it.

As I write, the agony of that loss comes welling up as if it were yesterday.

But time softens all. I had my glimpse into fairyland, the fairyland of love, hand in hand with Guy Tressinger, years ago. It is all over now, only the memory comes back to me with the " pain that is all but a pleasure."

But to go back to my wedding day.

Worn out with weeping and despair I fell into a deep, heavy sleep when day broke. From this I was soon awakened.

The ayah was standing over me, begging me to come quickly to baby, who was very ill.

In an instant I was by his cot, dazed and terrified.

There was no doubt of it. His wee face was blue and drawn. His tiny hands were tightly clenched with the thumbs turned inwards, while his little limbs twitched convulsively.

Even at this distance of time certain events of that long weary day stand out as distinctly as if it were yesterday, while the whole day is one long blue of agony, almost still too painful for me to describe in detail. It was a succession of hopes and fears. I hardly realised anything or felt real myself. I seemed a third person looking on at myself and baby.

At last, after what seemed an age of waiting, the doctor came. He looked very grave, and asked all manner of questions, which I answered as best I might. Then he gave his opinion.

"I'm afraid you won't save him."

He was only a young fellow, of the Army Medical Department.

He had never known heart-ache in his life. I am sure he did not in the least realise how his words fell like lead on my heart numbed with grief.

Then he offered to telegraph to Roger, adding he was afraid he would not get here in time. I let him do it, knowing all the while, though I hardly had the power to think, that it was quite impossible for Roger to get away at all.

Some time in the middle of the day (I did not keep count of hours) I was roused, as I sat by baby's cradle, from a stupor almost as great as that into which he had fallen, by Guy Tressinger's voice in the verandah, enquiring after me.

My heart gave a great bound. Here, at least, was a friend; some one to cling to in this great, overwhelming trouble.

But my next thought was one of horror. No, no, I would not, could not see him while Roger's baby—our baby—lay a-dying. It would be adding to my guilt. Was not, perhaps, this blow a punishment for having thought too much of him?

I rocked myself to and fro in my lonely grief over my darling's bed, putting Guy out of my thoughts.

When the doctor came again there was a slight rally. The fits ceased for a time. Still his face looked grey and drawn. You might have said a wax doll was lying there, you could hardly see his breathing.

Guy called again, and yet again, as the weary afternoon dragged on and the sun shone low in the verandah. The hotel was astir with people going for their evening walks and rides.

Then he sent in a note.

"My heart aches for you. Only tell me what I can do to help you.

"Yours ever,
"G. T."

Even while I was gazing at the note, a cry from the ayah drew my attention to the boy.

Alas! another convulsion had set in. His little face and limbs were twitching again.

When the doctor returned half an hour later, in tennis flannels, his bat under his arm, baby was quiet again, but he said another fit like that would carry him off.

The sun set. The short twilight came on. The room grew dark. Night fell—an inky, dark, moonless night.

With it came suddenly a great horror of loneliness, with a longing for mother, such as I had not felt since I was a child, and I awoke up in a fright in the dark and wanted comfort.

I could not cry. I had not shed a tear all day.

I sat there alone in the darkened room, wailing "Mother, mother!"

Oh! if she could only have heard! How she would have hurried to me, and suffered with me.

Baby lay in a state of coma. At times I thought him dead. I had to strain my ear so as to catch his breathing. I do not know how the time passed. They brought lights, they offered me food. I neither stirred nor answered.

Suddenly there was a sound of a man's footsteps clanking down the verandah. There was an altercation of voices outside; and then the curtain across the door was pushed aside, and Guy Tressinger entered in uniform.

"I have to go round the guards, past the telegraph office. Can I do anything for you?"

He stood hesitating in the doorway and looked beseechingly at me.

The sound of his voice roused me. I looked up. I met those eyes, which always influenced me so strangely, and they broke the spell.

I rose, and rushing towards him hid my face on his shoulder, and burst into wild, passionate weeping.

Even now I can feel his arms around me, and his hot kisses on my cheek as he murmured:

"My darling, my poor darling!"

There was a sound of approaching footsteps. He pushed me gently away. The doctor entered, and went over to baby's bed. I followed, and I think Guy left the room.

Baby was in another convulsion, worse than any of the preceding attacks. The doctor shook his head, and tried to get a few drops of medicine inside the tightly clenched little mouth. Then he shook his head again.

"I can do no more."

I bent over the cot and took baby up in my arms. I felt I would like to feel him there as long as I could.

Poor mite! His wide, blue eyes rolled back and became fixed.

The doctor went and looked out into the dark night.

How time passed I know not. I seemed stunned.

Suddenly there was a great commotion outside, a running down the verandah, a calling for the doctor. He went out, saying he would return directly.

I caught what they said to him outside.

"You're wanted at once, doctor. There's been an accident. Tressinger's fallen over the precipice. He was galloping wildly to the guard-room and his pony shied with him, and they both went over. A fatigue party has turned out to look for him. Come at once."

He looked in at the door, and must have seen from my face that I had heard all.

I motioned him away.

"Go, go at once. Don't delay."

And then I bent over my baby, praying as never in my life I had prayed before, not that he might be spared, but that I might be taken with him.

There was a long, long interval of silence and solitude.

Baby was quiet and still; such a feather-weight on my arm.

I heard a distant clock strike midnight, an owl screech, and a pack of jackals fill the night with their unearthly music, before the doctor returned.

When he did so, his face was white and set, and he seemed afraid to meet my eye.

I looked up at him.

There must have been command as well as entreaty in my face.

"Tell me," I asked in a harsh, hoarse voice, which sounded to me as if some one else was speaking.

He hesitated a moment.

"Captain Tressinger has met———"

"Tell me," I repeated.

His head drooped :

"He must have been killed instantly !"

Then he came across and bent over baby.

"Let me take him from you now. He does not need you any more."

MRS. CARAMEL'S BOW-WOW.

RIGHTLY or wrongly, people talked a good deal at the time, more even than people generally do talk in an Indian hill-station, which is saying a good deal. Mrs. Caramel was young, pretty, and attractive. She had met Herbert Aynsley one cold season at Punkahpore, and he had been much smitten. Then the following hot weather she had gone up to the hills alone for six months, to escape the heat, and he had taken leave and followed her thither. Up at that naughty little nook Nimree, among the rhododendrons and under the shadow of the mighty mountains, they were always together; for Mrs. Caramel found her own society unendurable. At the balls, after dancing eight or ten dances together, Aynsley would take her down to supper, and afterwards escort her home, under the stars, to her châlet-like cottage among the crags, where any one calling always found him hanging about very much at home. Then they were met in the twilight returning from long rides together, their ponies being led behind them while he helped her down the steep places. Long sunny afternoons he sculled her about the lake, and the great full Indian moon would beam down upon them idling about in canoes. Finally, it became an understood thing that neither would go to any dinner or picnic in which the other was not included, and that a seat must always be reserved for him everywhere next to her. To use the common Anglo-Indian slang, in short, Aynsley was acknowledged as Mrs. Caramel's " bow-wow."

Of course it was all a great pity, and Mrs. Caramel was very silly. But Herbert Aynsley was a good-looking young fellow, smarter and better groomed than the average competition-wallah. On the other hand, Colonel Caramel was fat and stupid, and years older than his wife. He did not seem to mind, if indeed he noticed, what was on everyone's tongue. One's own affairs are often more one's neighbour's business than one's own.

However, this had taken place some years ago, and now they were all at home. The Caramels had retired from the service. The Colonel had come into a little money, and had developed gouty tendencies; and they had settled down in a small house in Wessex, which had been left them with the property.

But the Herbert Aynsley friendship had not waned. As long as they were in India, though often widely separated by the exigencies of their respective services, he had generally contrived to get up to the hills for a little to Mrs. Caramel in summer, and to run over and see her at Christmas, or for an odd week now and again. It was quite an old story now, and people generally accepted it, as they do accept such friendship in the easy-going East. Aynsley was now home on sick-leave, and of course staying down in Wessex with the Caramels. But there was another reason for his being there besides his old penchant for Mrs. Caramel. This latter had grown decidedly stout; also she had lost some of her good looks, and presented the washed-out appearance of Anglo-Indian beauties when viewed in contrast with their fresher English sisters. Aynsley was getting a little tired of her. Then the doctors had told him he ought not to go back to India again ; but alas ! he was overwhelmed with debts, the result of years of extravagance. What was to be done ? Mrs. Caramel was fully alive to the state of affairs. Like a wise woman, she seized the bull by the horns, and determined to get him married. Like the true friend she was, with the utmost devotion she discovered an heiress for him.

The McKinlay's widow and only daughter lived at the big house, Ashleigh Manor, only a stone's throw from the Caramel's little place. Old McKinlay had made a large fortune in business, bought the property, and then died. His only surviving child was Caroline, aged nineteen—just the girl Mrs. Caramel wanted to get hold of for Aynsley. She was a thoroughly good girl this Caroline McKinlay : very strictly brought up, and gentle and loving. She would make him a harmless, commonplace sort of wife. Then she had 8000*l*. a year. A further advantage was that she was decidedly plain, with sandy hair, pale eyes, and a bad complexion—not at all the sort of girl to exercise much influence over a man like Aynsley ; and Mrs. Caramel was not in the least afraid of his getting too fond of her. Her mother was a tall, angular, sharp-featured Scotch-woman, who had married McKinlay in his early obscure days, and had not and never would accommodate herself entirely to her improved position. She was a strong Presbyterian, and took an austere view of life; but in deference to her position as mistress of Ashleigh Manor, she condescended on Sundays to occupy the great square pew in the village church, which went with the big house.

Aynsley's suit had progressed charmingly. All that beautiful month of August he had laid siege to the heiress's heart. He was to her as a god descended from Olympus; she had met very few men, and none to be compared to him. In the meantime, Mrs. Caramel, with her honeyed little ways, had quite captivated the mamma. In fact, she had obtained so much influence over that lady, who imagined her the "glass of fashion and the mould of form," that she had actually persuaded her to issue invitations for a grand garden party (dances Mrs. McKinlay deemed a snare of the Evil One), to commemorate Caroline's nineteenth birthday, when the house should be thrown open for the first time since the old man's death. At this party Mrs. Caramel intended that Aynsley should lay the copingstone on her plans by proposing to the heiress.

The evening before this great event Mrs. Caramel sat on her little lawn, after tennis was over, dispensing tea, or rather brandy-and-soda, and good advice simultaneously, to Aynsley, who lay on his back on the grass, looking very handsome in his flannels, and contemplating lazily the little spiral curls of smoke he puffed up into the air.

"You're really very lazy to-night, Bertie," she remarked from the depths of a low basket chair; "I'm sure you're not attending even to what I am saying to you. You must really make up your mind—that is, if you have any to make up, which I almost begin to doubt—as to when you are going to do it. Is it to be when you give her the bouquet (it will be down from Covent Garden the first thing to-morrow morning), or shall it come off in the evening, after everyone has left? I could bring her into the garden and make an opportunity for you. Now tell me, what am I to do?"

"I really don't know, and I'm sure I don't care," drawled Herbert. "By Jove! it's really an awful thought that by this time to-morrow a fellow may not be his own master any longer! And then there's that old canting hag of a mother, too! I shall belong half to her, I suppose."

"Really, Herbert, you're very exasperating to-night," pouted Mrs. Caramel. "Here am I arranging all this for you, and you are too lazy even to decide, much less to say thank you. Why, I suppose," she sighed, "you never even give me a thought in the matter. Perhaps this is the last evening I shall even be allowed to call you 'Bertie,' for instance, after all these years." And her handkerchief went up to her pretty blue eyes.

"Come, come, little woman," said Herbert soothingly, rousing himself as he spoke. "That's all nonsense, you know. We shall always be the same to each other whatever happens; you know that. Come along, and let's have a row on the river before dinner." And he put his arm in hers and led her away.

The next day was the garden-party. A bright afternoon, and the place looked its best. Not so Caroline McKinlay, tortured with hopes and fears as to Aynsley's intentions; and then, as Mrs. Caramel charitably remarked, she never looked well in white. There were tennis-nets on the lawns, the Militia band under the trees. Tents with refreshments and little umbrella-tents were dotted about picturesquely. The flower-garden was a blaze of colour, ditto the toilettes of the guests. All the world of Wessex was there, many more than Mrs. McKinlay knew the names of; for in the country we visit the houses and not the people who live in them, and Ashleigh Manor had always been a visitable house. People, too, had brought friends with them, people they had staying in their houses; for had not the words "and party" been added to the name on each card when Mrs. Caramel had superintended the sending out of the invitations?

The shadows of the grand old elms were lengthening over the tennis-courts. Mrs. McKinlay was standing rather solitary and unnoticed among the crowd, who all seemed to know each other so much better than she knew them. Suddenly she caught a fragment of a conversation:

"Well, I declare! If that is not that Mrs. Caramel!"

The speaker was Mrs. General Crabtree, just home from India. (The Crabtrees are a fine old "qui-hai" family, with ramifications in both services, scattered all over India. You must surely, dear reader, have met one or other of them. They have all a touch of the tar-brush; but people in England don't mind that.)

Somebody rejoined, " Yes, there she is, to be sure, in pink. How stout she's got !"

" Yes, indeed ; and how gone off ! I always said her looks wouldn't last. And do look ! There's Herbert Aynsley with her ! Only fancy, my dear, *that* going on still ! And at home here; how shocking ! I wonder that old fool Caramel has not divorced her long ago. O, how *do* you do, my *dear* Mr. Aynsley ? " (with effusion.) " Who would have thought of meeting you here ? " &c.

A little later on, while handing her a cup of tea, Herbert whispers to Mrs. Caramel, " Here's bad luck ! That old black cat, Mother Crabtree, has turned up. I only hope she doesn't make mischief."

Mrs. Caramel turns rather white under her rouge, for Mrs. Crabtree is one of those dear Indian friends of hers she is always talking about, whom she did not so much care about meeting.

An hour later and the twilight is falling on the now deserted gardens. The carriages are rolling away down the avenue—the lordly barouche of the country magnate, the parsonical wagonette, the drag from the barracks, and the humble hired fly from the neighbouring town. As Mrs. Caramel drives off she casts an admiring glance at the stately old pile and the finely timbered park.

" Dear fellow ! It will be very nice to have him settled so near. It's a nice place, and they shall give a big ball."

Herbert Aynsley and Caroline McKinlay are strolling up and down the Beech Walk, out of earshot of the servants who are clearing the tents and taking down the nets. It is already dusk under the trees ; but he can mark her pale cheeks crimson and her head bend lower and lower as he pours into her ears those sweet words of love which she now hears for the first time, and which are so familiar to him from long practice. At the end of the walk he stops, bends over her, and takes her unresisting hand. His arm steals round her waist.

"Caroline!—may I call you Caroline?—say you care for me! Say you will be my wife?"

He looks so handsome; those dark eyes of his pierce her very soul. For all answer she lets her head fall on his shoulder, and, as he kisses her, love transfigures her face and makes her almost pretty. Then she frees herself and runs away from him, into the shadow and so up to the house, and hides herself in her own room —the happiest girl in England.

Aynsley lights a cigar deliberately and strolls back leisurely across the darkening park to report himself to Mrs. Caramel. In the avenue a carriage passes him. It contains Mrs. Crabtree, who had been detained awhile by her hostess.

"I want a few words wi' ye privately," had pleaded Mrs. McKinlay, leading her into the large library, which was furnished, as was all the house, by some eminent London upholsterer. The walls were lined with books in fine calf bindings, books which had never been opened, while busts of unknown celebrities stood sentinel in the corner.

"I saw ye speaking wi' that Mr. Aynsley," continued Mrs. McKinlay, standing erect before her visitor, her hands tightly clasped, and her face wearing an anxious look, while her native Doric came out strong. "For pity's sake tell me if ye ken anything wrong about him, for he's after my bairn."

Thus adjured, and nothing loth, Mrs. Crabtree opens the flood-gates of her store of gossip and scandal, adding notes and comments and embroideries various. It was dusk before her recital was ended, and she drove off in a benign frame of mind, with a sense of having done her duty, leaving her hostess rocking herself to and fro in her grief in the dark library.

A few hours later she stands with arms folded and lips pursed by her daughter's bedside. "Has he spake to ye, chield?" she asks sternly.

Caroline from her pillows confesses he *has* spoken, but does not think it necessary to mention the kiss.

"Weel, then, I tell ye that he's a verra bad young man. We've been cherishing vipers in our bosom, and ye'd better think no more about him, for ye shall never set eyes on him agin!"

Next morning, when Aynsley walks over to the Manor, for the first time he is denied admittance, and cannot catch a glimpse of either mother or daughter. Hardly has he returned, and is discussing with his fellow-conspirator what this may mean, than a letter is brought him, as he is sitting in Mrs. Caramel's pretty little morning room. Aynsley reads the letter, blurts out an oath, and tossing it over to Mrs. Caramel, stalks lugubriously out of the French window, with his hands in his pockets. This is the letter:

"Sir,—From inquiries I have made respecting your character, I must beg to decline, on my daughter's behalf, as her parent and guardian, the offer of marriage you have made her, and beg that all acquaintance between us cease from this out.—Yours faithfully,

"JANET MCKINLAY."

In her anxiety not to be misunderstood, the poor woman had sat up half the night writing and re-writing this epistle.

Mrs. Caramel flew into the garden after the rejected one. She laid her hand on his shoulder. "O Bertie!" she began.

He shrank from her with a scowl. "Damn you!" he muttered. "If it had not been for my fooling with you, this wouldn't have happened. What the devil am I to do now, I should like to know?" And he turned away from her.

That afternoon he packed his portmanteau, and took the train to town, and Mrs. Caramel has never seen him or heard from him since.

Aynsley's leave was just up, and he had to return to India or starve. On his arrival he found himself posted to that delightful station Guramghur, a dull little hole, blest with a feverish reputation, and where his social charms were quite thrown away, as there was not a lady in the place.

Down in Wessex, Caroline, a few years after, marries the very High Church curate; and when she has a thought to spare from him and her many babies, can think of Aynsley without even a sigh.

But the doors of Ashleigh Manor are closed for ever to Mrs. Caramel, and she finds the neighbourhood looks shyly upon her (for we are nothing if not respectable down in Wessex); and old Caramel's temper is often very bad with the gout.

THE TABLES TURNED.

"I'M sure it's true! I saw the names in the list of passengers by the *Hydaspes*, and the old bearer told my ayah that there was a 'mem-sahib' coming."

Mrs. Commissioner de Forret and Mrs. General Gupper were discussing in the ladies' reading-room of the club at the Indian station of Noluck the surprising intelligence that was electrifying the community.

There was no longer any doubt about it. Mr. Hurrell, the judge, who had gone home to England on three months' privilege leave, was returning with a wife. It was astonishing, incredible!

Let the European reader at once dissociate any idea of the venerable majesty of the law with an Indian judge. Specimens are to be found as young as briefless barristers nearer the shadow of the Law Courts. One has obtained undying fame as a polo-player, and another as a pig-sticker. Mr. Hurrell emulated none of these. His outward man was of uncertain age, heavy-looking and plain. But the society of the South-Eastern Provinces, in the commission of which he was, cherished him as one of her brightest ornaments. As a wit and a *raconteur* he was sought for at every big and little dinner. Noluck, which had now rejoiced in the light of his countenance for some months, was—especially the female part of it—in despair.

Not that any of the unattached had ever in their wildest dreams aspired to marrying him. No one ever could associate Mr. Hurrell and marriage together. But of his flirting capabilities there was no end.

There was mourning in the messes and clubs—Hurrell was such good company. Both sexes sighed for the snug little dinners (such cooking, such stories !) which would now be things of the past.

They arrived (yes, it was they, beyond a doubt), and the following day she loomed, large and fair and placid, upon the horizon of the Noluck world, driving up the Mall in the judicial barouche, with red-turbaned grooms armed with yaks' tails whisking the flies off her golden tresses.

Two days later Mr. Hurrell took her round, calling, after the good old Indian custom, in the very heat of the day, between twelve and two. Society was instantly divided in its opinions about her. The women were captivated by her new clothes. (Paris, you may be quite sure, said Mrs. General Gupper, whose frocks were all made by a cross-legged tailor in the verandah.) The men, on the other hand, were taken with this beautiful, calm, Juno-like creature, with exquisite complexion, and speaking eyes, languishing under half-lowered lids. And such a neck and shoulders !

" Only much too much of a good thing, I should say," sneered Mrs. Commissioner de Forret, after a big dinner she had given in the Hurrells' honour, and on whom the Indian climate has a disintegrating effect.

But as the men predominated over the other sex in Noluck—as, indeed, they do everywhere in Indian society —Mrs. Hurrell had a success, especially among the younger men, who, as a rule, like well-ripened charms.

Another point in her favour, and which went far towards disarming the women, was the discovery that Mr. Hurrell was in nowise deteriorated by marriage. His wings were not in the least clipped—in fact, he soared to flights as brilliant as before, or more so. The little dinners were resumed. His fair friends found themselves as welcome as ever, while all the world was chuckling over the last new funny story that Hurrell had brought out from home.

Of course, as regarded Hurrell, all this was admired and applauded. With the usual immunity of his sex, he might commit larceny over any quantity of quadrupeds. But woe betide madame if the Mrs. Grundys, the self-constituted lord chamberlains and guardians of the morals of Noluck, had found her even hovering near the stable gate.

But no fear. Mrs. Hurrell, with exquisite seamanship, trimmed her sails precisely so as to float as near the wind as possible, and yet so as not to raise the faintest breeze which might flutter the dovecots of Noluck. If there is anything in the old proverb about safety in numbers, Mrs. Hurrell was as safe as a church. But then a pretty woman has no difficulty about numbers in India, which is always the flirt's happy hunting ground.

But as the merry month of May drew near apace, Noluck (in the physical meaning of the word alone, be it quite understood) grew too hot for her. Houses were being taken in the hills, the feminine portion of the European population was packing up, and men's thoughts turned to the slaying of pigs, and of leave home.

Naturally Mr Hurrell was entitled to no leave: his thoughts ran on club hot-weather whist. But a man would have been a brute who should condemn a complexion like Mrs. Hurrell's to the shrivelling effects of the hot weather. Mrs. Hurrell went to the hills.

There must be something very enervating morally as well as physically, to the European constitution in the atmosphere of that naughty little nook among the rhododendrons, Simree. A few hundred English men and women, with mostly nothing to do, are crowded together over a few square miles of mountain side for weeks on end as on a large ship—and we all know who it is who then sets to work, chuckling, to provide mischief for the idlers. But perhaps, if Mephistopheles were to run up thither for a few days from the Lyceum, he would return with a melancholy arching of his eyebrows and declare the place too bad for him.

When Philip Avebury, a subaltern of the Dumbartonshire Regiment, was sent up to Simree, on two months' leave, after a bad attack of fever, his evil star led him to put up at the Highcliffe Hotel. This was the very head-quarters of all the fun and the racket and the noisiness and the naughtiness of Simree—in fact, it had been honoured with a little stanza all to itself by the local Bunthorne when the Amateur Dramatic Company put "Patience" on the boards. It ran thus:—

> A Highcliffe Hotel young man,
> A kiss-and-don't-tell young man,
> A take 'em to Morrison's and feed 'em on bonbons,
> A do-himself-wel young man.

Philip Avebury was a dark-eyed, melancholy youth, of pensive appearance and slightly artistic tendencies, and with plenty of money and good prospects. He posed as the interesting invalid. As such it was, of course, very much better for him that he should ride out quietly by the side of Mrs. Hurrell's palanquin, through quiet ravines and along lonely mountain-paths, than tire himself over cricket or tennis with the giddy throng by the Assembly Rooms. They said they were collecting butterflies, of which gorgeous specimens are to be found in the Himalayas. But Mrs. Hurrell had made rather a good collection of her own, among the human specimens, before Philip Avebury's arrival. But she put them all away now, and devoted herself to helping him.

Mrs. General Gupper was spending a rather dull hot weather at Noluck. The station was very empty, save of men. There was no one to talk about. Imagine her delight when the post brought her a real ripe bit of scandal from her friend Mrs. de Ferret at Simree.

"I should never have believed it—no, never! But it's perfectly true. Colonel Smith met them riding down the hill together to the railways as he came up, and the woman actually bowed. Poor, dear Mr. Hurrell, I quite feel for him! Such a blow! And they say she hasn't paid for a thing in Simree, and has bills all over the place; and you know how she dresses! That Mr. Avebury is certainly a very good-looking young man, I must say. People say they've gone to Australia, and that he has sent in his papers. Of course he'd be obliged to : the Dumbartonshire couldn't stand it. Well, I am surprised! But it really serves Mr. Hurrell right. At his time of life, and with his knowledge of women, how could he——?" &c.

The story was all over the north of India in a few days, for Hurrell was a well-known man. With amendments and embroideries various it grew and grew, forming a pleasant topic of conversation now the rains had set in and every one's spirits languished. It had been such a flagrant, open, and above-board elopement. Now in India great virtue is attached to a rider locally added to the seventh commandment " if thou be found out."

But this affair was done in the light of day. There was not even any finding out required (worse luck for the gossips). Under the circumstances, it was naturally irresistible for the residents of Simree to have a fling at the culprit, notwithstanding the fact that many of them resided in glass houses.

How Mr. Hurrell took it—whether it was indeed true that he had rushed up to Simree on the first hint of the business—that the two *dâk gharrys* had met *en route* at a change of horses, and that Mrs. H. had had to lean back in her carriage to avoid being recognised by her husband—Noluck never knew; for just at this crisis the Goddess of Red Tape who presides over the Government of India swooped down upon him and carried him off in her peculiarly sudden and unmeaning fashion, to officiate for somebody or other somewhere else.

En revanche, at the beginning of the cold weather, with the departure of the punkah-coolies, the advent of the globe-trotters, and the return of the dwellers in the hills, Noluck and Mrs. de Ferret experienced a really startling sensation. The Dumbartonshire Regiment marched in to relieve the Duchess of Devonshire's Scilly Highlanders, and with them came Lieutenant Philip Avebury, and with Lieutenant Avebury came— Mrs. Hurrell!

Society at Noluck, including, of course, everybody who had known her there, and those who had been with her up at Simree, drew their virtuous garments around them, and passed her by on the other side.

A great personage, who was there playing at soldiering in the East, and as such ruled supreme in Noluck cantonments as brigadier-general, was much scandalised and perturbed. Being himself a pattern of domestic virtue in a family which, both in the present and past generations, had not been noted for the same (though his mother had always been a great stickler for propriety), he felt himself bound to send for Avebury, and remonstrate with him on the presence of Mrs. Hurrell in his bungalow. If he could only have seen how the yellow-haired one laughed, when she read the official letter delivered in hot haste by the orderly!

Avebury arrayed himself in uniform and sword, and cantered leisurely down to the General's bungalow. He was a man of few words, and the latter had to do all the talking, which embarrassed him, as he was not used to giving wiggings.

"Mr. Avebury—um—I have sent for you—um—to remonstrate with you on the presence—um—um. I have been creditably informed that you have—um—a lady—um—living with you—um, um—a Mrs. Hurrell——"

"Pardon me, sir, not Mrs. Hurrell."

"What do you mean, sir?—the wife of Mr. Hurrell, the judge—I am—um—not aware that he has instituted any—um—divorce proceedings—um——"

"No, sir," replied Avebury quietly. "He couldn't do that!"

"How—a—what? Please explain, Mr. Avebury."

"Well, sir, she was never his wife to divorce——"

"Not his wife! What do you mean? Who is she?"

"Mine, sir, now. We were married last month."

A POLO SMASH.

"NOT married? Not Brantwood? Never!"

The Crimson Cuirassiers were sitting at mess, a long and glittering array of gold lace-laden human beings, while the tables groaned under trophies of silver plate. It was Mackenzie, the adjutant, who had announced this overwhelming piece of news.

"What's your authority, Mac?" cried a voice from the other end of the table.

"No one less than Brandy himself," replied Mackenzie. "Got a letter from him by mail—English letters just in, you know!"

"By George, then, I've won my bet!" continued the speaker with exultation. "Had a pony on with him as to which of us wouldn't be married first. Waiter, bring a magnum of champagne."

"And who's the lucky one?" asked another voice. that of the sub., who was susceptible and always in love.

A cynical snigger went round the table.

"Oh! a swell," replied the oracle. "A Lady Somebody Something—Sybil, I think—can't remember: Why, confound it, Penheale, I wish you'd be more careful, man."

For Geoffrey Penheale, sitting next the adjutant, had started violently, and upset the latter's claret over his mess overalls.

"Awfully sorry, old man," rejoined the other, mopping his victim up with his napkin. "Show me Brandy's letter, will you, after dinner?"

"It's at my bungalow. Come back with me this evening, and I will."

Penheale did look in at Mackenzie's bungalow as he went to bed, and came out a sadder and a wiser man.

The next mail's newspapers brought a flaming account of the marriage, by a bishop or two, of Major the Hon. Basil Brantwood, of the Crimson Cuirassiers, with Lady Sybil, daughter of the Earl of Tallboys. But when Geoffrey Penheale had read every word of it in the *Morning Post*, not even omitting the description of the bridesmaids' dresses, he went back to the bare whitewashed barn where he lived, and, lighting a fusee solemnly committed to the flames on the tiles of the verandah, for lack of a fireplace, a packet of letters in a woman's hand, and a lock of hair. Then he applied for three days' leave, and went out on a shooting expedition all by himself. But he made a very poor bag.

In due course the P. and O. steamer brought Major Brantwood back to the "shiny" and to the bosom of his regiment. Matrimony had evidently produced no alteration in him. He was as small and lean and dapper, as cynical and reserved and unpleasant as ever. His little moustache was as elaborately waxed as if it had never been out of cosmetique since he started home: the *chaussure* of those small feet—of which he was so justly proud—was as irreproachable as the best

Bond Street bootmaker could turn them out. He came and dined at mess the first night as usual (Lady Sybil was tired, he said, with her journey), and before he left the table had withered up each individual thereat with some smart neat cutting thing he said, and made every one feel very uncomfortable.

The next day was Sunday. As a rule, the Crimson Cuirassiers could not be said to be inveterate church-goers. But upon the Sabbath in question they were loth to leave their religious duties to the orderly officer told off to take the men to church, and turned up to a man—to see Lady Sybil.

And they saw—a pale, slim slip of a girl, half Brantwood's age, with a wealth of dark hair and large, sad grey eyes.

"And such a dowd!" quoth Mrs. Wildinge, wife of the captain of that name, and who "lived up to it," as the æsthetes say of blue china. "Well, if I were an earl's daughter, and had just had a trousseau, I'd have smarter frocks than that!"

And no one doubted it of Mrs. Wildinge. But then the number and the magnificence of her gowns were a standing puzzle to her acquaintance, most of all to her husband, who was simple-minded, and invariably impecunious.

Now, there had been much wondering among the Crimson Cuirassiers as to how Mrs. W. would take Brantwood's marriage. Not that the latter had ever been guilty of transgressing that eleventh commandment which holds good in all crack corps, and which runs "Thou shalt not flirt with thy brother-officer's wife."

But then Captain Wildinge had only been transferred, on promotion, to the Cuirassiers a short while before, and there was a time—not a hundred years ago—when Major Brantwood and Mrs. Wildinge had been fast friends all through one festive season at merry Mussoorie, in the hills.

Geoffrey Penheale had been remiss in his attendance at church, and had not been among the throng to whom Major Brantwood introduced his bride, under the portico after service, while the Cuirassiers swung away back to barracks to the sound of merry music. It was only on the polo ground next day that Penheale met Lady Sybil.

Brantwood was not playing, for of course he had not yet got any ponies together; he had driven his wife down in a pony-cart while the game was going on. When it ended, and some fellows sauntered up to her to chat, Brantwood was among those who was found refreshing himself at the "peg" table spread under the mango-tree for thirsty players. Penheale was next him, clad in red-and-white striped polo jersey, jaunty cap, and white breeches and boots, similarly engaged.

"Here, Penheale, don't think you know my wife!" and the major, with the pride of the possessor of a new toy, seized Penheale by the arm and dragged him up to the pony-cart.

"Sybil—here—let me introduce Penheale."

Every vestige of colour faded from Lady Sybil's cheek as she turned round and saw Penheale before her. The latter became as white as his nether garments, and dropped his eyes.

"What's the matter, dear Lady Sybil?" asked a silvery voice at her side. "You look as if you were going to faint. Not used to the heat, I suppose. Do some one get her a 'peg'—O but you must, just a weak one!"

The observant speaker was Mrs. Wildinge, on her little chestnut Arab, who had malevolently watched for some time Lady Sybil monopolising all the men's attention.

Three days afterwards Geoffrey Penheale, who had put down his name to go in for a garrison class course at a station at some distance soon after hearing of Brantwood's marriage, departed, to go, as it were, to school again. Every one missed him; he was a very popular fellow.

It was two months before he came back to the regiment, to find Lady Sybil looking paler and sadder than ever.

The next day the Crimson Cuirassiers gave a dance to the royal duke, who, in guise of divisional major-general, had come over to inspect them. The intoxication of the brilliant scene, the glamour of the soul-stirring waltzes, got into Penheale's head. Before he almost knew what he was doing, he had asked Lady Sybil, ethereal-looking in her billowy white tulle, for a dance.

The delirium of feeling her once more in his arms unloosed his tongue, as a few minutes later they found themselves sitting alone in the dim verandah, the music hushed, and the moonlit garden stretched out before them.

"Sybil! Sybil!" he asked hoarsely and bitterly, "how could you?"

All answer was a sob.

"Is this your love, your faith?"

The tears fell fast on the billowy white tulle.

"Oh! answer me, Sybil. Surely I deserve—surely I've a right to know."

"Oh! Geoffrey," she broke out, in agony—"oh! you misjudge me terribly. If you but knew—how they drove me to it. Mamma said it was such a good match; papa is so hard up; there are so many of us girls; they left me no peace till I accepted him. How could I guess I was to meet you?"

"I had exchanged, to get away out of England. I could not bear my life after your people dismissed me, but I remained true, Sybil, all this while. I've never thought even of any one else!"

He was torturing her, and she gave a little cry of pain.

"Oh, Geoffrey, if you only knew! I've never thought of any one else day and night—— Oh, God, what am I saying, But it's true, it's true!"

She buried her face in her hands and sobbed aloud. Only the sound of her weeping broke the stillness, till the music suddenly began again and recalled them to themselves.

Sybil started up and recovered herself with a mighty effort, and as she did so Penheale's self-control gave way. He caught her in his arms, and, pressing her lips to his, whispered—

"Forgive me, my darling!"

The next minute they had passed out into the lighted ball-room, and, after a safe interval, the form of Mrs. Wildinge arose from an armchair in a dark corner, where she had been resting

"Very pretty!" she said to herself—"very pretty! And, upon my word, very good for such a young and artless beginner. Master Brandy, you've got a wife worthy of you!"

A few days later that officer was detailed for a general court-martial at a station at some distance. Instead of lasting only two or three days, the trial, which was an important one, dragged on, and detained him much longer than he expected. To compensate him for the detention, however, he had the agreeable excitement of receiving by post an anonymous letter, which ran thus:—

"You had better look after your wife and Geoffrey P, If, for instance, the trial happened to be over in time for you to take the train which arrives at your station late in the evening, and you accidentally happened to walk up to your bungalow quietly, you might see and hear something to your advantage—or otherwise."

I suppose Major Brantwood would hardly have been human if in the end, after many *pros* and *cons*, he had not profited by this advice. An old poacher makes a very good gamekeeper, and with him a hint was enough. He did come by the last train, and he did walk up from the station, a most unprecedented occurrence in a land where no one ever walks who can drive, and a most unusual thing for a man with Major Brantwood's neat boots to do on the dusty Indian roads.

Whether the game was worth the candle, or the scandal worth his little game, no one ever knew, for the *chokedar*, or watchman, was sound asleep, as in duty bound, in one corner of the verandah, and the servants were all in bed for the night in their little row of mud hovels in one corner of the compound.

Mrs. Wildinge, who, of course, had penned the anonymous letter, would have given her eyes to find out if she had done any harm or not; but next day a terrible event turned her thoughts in quite a different direction.

This event was none other than that dreadful polo accident which threw such a gloom over the Cuirassiers.

The polo ground, after the manner of polo grounds in India at that season, was simply a sea of dust when it had been played on for a little while. A pillar of cloud accompanied the players as they scurried over the ground, and hid them from the spectators, and often from each other.

No one ever knew quite what happened. Two or three were riding for the ball. The dust was so thick you couldn't see a yard in front of you. Some one crossed, or some one came up off side. No one knew. But there was a terrible collision; and when the dust cleared off Brantwood was seen slowly picking himself up. But Geoffrey Penheale lay motionless on the ground. It was fracture of the skull, the doctors said, and he never spoke again, and died in the night.

Brantwood appeared more perturbed by the accident than any one had ever seen him by anything before. In fact, he seemed to feel it more than he did his wife's death, which took place, not many weeks after, suddenly of cholera, one of those solitary sporadic cases which crop up occasionally in even the best-sanitated stations.

AFTER THE WILY BOAR.

It was getting very hot. Never mind what the glass stood at in the verandah at noon; it was too hot to go out and see. The voice of the brain fever bird was once more heard in the land, its agonising prolonged three notes proclaiming the hot weather is nigh. Houses were being taken in the hill stations, and the feminine portion of the population was packing up.

But my breast was stirred by no dreams of hill flirtations, of Cashmere big game, or of leave home. I was on pigsticking bent, and not being exactly of a frugal mind, I had set myself up well with the noble animal and had entered the horse I fancied most for the Bulampore Tent Club Cup.

The sun was low in the western sky as I rode out towards the camp of meeting, from a large station sacred in the British mind to one of the saddest memories of the Mutiny times. My way lay through the ruins of former cantonments, along dusty, tree-bordered highways, along which flocks of goats and cows were being driven in from pasture (save the mark!) Then I struck across country, past emerald wheat crops and sun-baked plain, and by clusters of mud huts yclept villages, to which, as their sanitary arrangements were not all that could be desired, I gave a wide berth. Here and there a Government-planted rectangular group of mango trees broke the level flat.

AFTER THE WILY BOAR.

Presently I reached the sacred river, and rode along the high sand-banks it throws up in the rains. All the way I had met nothing but crows and coolies, but then, like snakes and the cholera, these we have always with us in India. Once on a plain I had fancied I descried a herd of black buck among the low scrub, and now on the river sands I disturbed three pariah dogs quarrelling over the body of a defunct Hindoo, that Mother Ganges had rejected from her sacred bosom.

The sun had set rapidly in a cloudless cadmium sky, and the short Indian twilight was coming on, bringing with it a perceptible lowering of the temperature. So I hurried the polo pony I was riding into a hand canter and gained the camp.

Under the auspices of an indefatigable secretary, a cluster of white tabernacles had arisen under the grateful shades of a mango grove. In the midst stood the mess-tent. On the outskirts of the grove everybody's horses were tethered in lines, with head and heel ropes. Their single blanket formed their manger by day, and a single bucket and brush their toilet requisites. Their two attendants slept and ate by their side, and their luggage was of quite an elementary description.

A smaller wood a couple of hundred yards further off was given over to the married camp. There the ladies were out of earshot of the midnight revelry which is apt to disturb the bats in our camp. Also it shows how we discourage the feminine element altogether. Some of the talkative sex would indeed view the sport from the *howdah* of an elephant on the morrow, but as yet none will show us the way. I never heard of a woman carrying a spear and pigsticking. Here is an opening for the shrieking sisterhood.

Before I turned in for my ante-prandial tub, *more* India, I went to have a look at the nags. As is usually the case, they had marched hither. It is really odd in India how we entrust a valuable animal to an utterly faithless native and despatch him to proceed his stages of ten miles a day for days and even weeks, through a country devoid of inns and unknown to the groom. He turns up somehow, however, probably having stolen and eaten a good deal of the horse's forage and pocketed some of the rupees provided for the latter's subsistence, and the horse appears very little the worse for it.

The evening was oppressed with a sense of the importance of the morrow. After dinner, the forty horses (for it is the horses, not the riders, who enter for the Cup, the horses being frequently not ridden by their owners), were drawn by lot into ten heats of four each. Then when we had greeted old friends and acquaintances, discussed our own and everyone else's animals, and perhaps done a bit of horse-dealing, and told not a few lies, we think about bed.

Not but what it seems a pity. The night is still, starry, and balmy as only an Indian night can be. The camp is very still, and as we throw away the end of a cigar, before we turn in, only a pariah bays from a neighbouring village, or a jackal howls in the distance. A disturbed owl in the mango tree above wanted to know what it all meant, but I didn't enlighten him, and sought such repose upon my curtainless "charpoy" as the mosquitos would allow me.

"Sahib, sahib, half six has struck. Sahib, sahib!"

The old bearer mumbled imploringly in my ear. I consigned him to all sorts of dreadful places, but with a perseverance born of long experience he went at it again. In an inconceivably short space of time he had got me up and dressed me, and booted and spurred I was sipping my morning tea at the door of the tent. The crows are up, though the sun is scarcely so. It must, indeed, be an early worm that can circumvent the Indian crows. There is much shouting at and for servants, and some bad language going on in the tents around. Tempers are not sweet at 7 A.M.

Gradually everyone emerges. We are indeed a motley crew, for every class of the European population in India is represented. There is one civilian, a full-blown commissioner, whom everyone, notwithstanding, calls "Jim." Five and twenty years in the "shiny" have not dimmed his geniality and his love of sport, and though it has somewhat reduced his spare little form, we shall presently see him going as well as anyone. The climate has had an opposite effect upon his equally sporting colleague, whose broad back looms before me upon a country-bred cob. Colonels are there and noisy subalterns, rising "competition-wallahs," and sporting police officers, with a detective's eye on a pig. Trade is not unrepresented, and a neighbouring rajah, who owns and has entered some fine Arabs, comes out to view the sport on a wonderfully caparisoned steed.

The costumes are as varied as the riders. Some men go in for a turban, some for a mushroom-shaped pith hat, while some wear a soldier's helmet with a curtain hanging down over the nape of the neck to protect them from the sun. Some men ride in thin tweed or flannel coats, some in white drill or drab-coloured " karkee" cotton, some wear merely a flannel shirt, while others are padded across the shoulders and down the spine as a cricketer pads his legs. But one and all grasp a stout male bamboo, six feet six inches long, weighted with lead at one end, and tipped at the other with a fine steel head.

As various, too, are the mounts. Smart-looking little country or stud-breds, with, perhaps, queer tempers and man-eating propensities; languid-looking stumbling Arabs, who look a pig in the white of the eye, as the French say ; and grand big Walers (Australians) standing sixteen hands high, like English hunters and splendid fencers, but alas, not equally staunch to pig !

There was a general move towards the home preserve which is to be drawn first. It was a large patch of grass jungle, tall elephant grass, kept sacred for this big meet. The sportsmen drew off on either side to the shelter of two small villages, and the hundreds of native beaters and the long line of elephants were turned into covert.

Those who were drawn in the first heat tightened their girths and sat lance in rest. We, whose turn was not yet come, lit our cigars. To each party was an umpire.

AFTER THE WILY BOAR.

Nearer and nearer down the jungle came the roar of the beaters' cries through the fresh morning air. We could see the tall grass waving where the elephants were crashing through. The game began to break covert: Pea-fowl flew screeching away over our heads, and a herd of startled black buck leapt wildly away across the open, in prodigious bounds. Hares ran under our very horses' feet, and quail and partridge whirred by unnoticed.

Suddenly a large, dark mass lollopped quietly away from a corner of the jungle. No one stirred till he had got a good start, and the umpire shouted "ride!"

In an instant four riders were after the boar. One was on a Waler, two on Arabs, and the fourth was that civilian with whom the climate agreed so well, mounted on his cob. But the Waler had the pace, and got up with the pig first. Looking on at the horse laying himself out at a racing gallop, and the pig "gallumping awkwardly on just ahead," one failed to understand how the former did not gain on him. But the way the pig negotiated an eight-foot chain in his stride showed how good the pace really was.

But piggy, getting blown perhaps, after a good, straight run across the plain, "jinked" to the left, and the Waler could not or would not turn smartly enough. This let in one of the Arabs. The boar led him over a castor-oil field, with a crop some ten feet high, which taken externally brought his rider to grief. The Waler came up again, and rattled the pig into a corn crop. But the Waler sheered off just as his rider got alongside with his spear down for a thrust. The pig "jinked" across under the horse's nose, and ran almost between the legs of the country-bred with the heavy-weight, who, disregarding any interference on the part of the society for suppressing cruelty to animals, turned the cob round upon him in a moment, and took first spear off him in the quarters.

While this run was proceeding, several other pig had broken covert, and other parties had been despatched after them. At a big meeting like this for the Cup, sows are frequently ridden as well as boars, though this is not the case in everyday sport. Some of the weaker sex, however, led their pursuers a fine dance, and one old lady squatted down defiantly in a path of corn, and charged like a boar. Of course it is the first spear that counts, but in most cases the pig were polished off, some few escaping, we hope, to fight another day. Some showed fight; one grey old fellow, badly wounded, sat himself down under a thorn bush, foaming at the mouth and charging desperately, till an individual, with more pluck than discretion, dismounted and gave him his quietus by a lucky shot between the shoulders.

My turn came unexpectedly; I never have any luck. My stable companions were on Arabs too, and a long stern chase was looked for. But I got a bad start, and for some time only rode after the others for lack of seeing the boar. Then there ensued a hitch and an incoherency in a wheat crop. The pig had squatted. Some one spotted him and whoo-whooped on my right, and before I was aware, a huge black mass thirty-three inches at shoulder, with bristles erect, and murderous-looking tusks, bore down upon me.

"Steady, old boy!" as I set the little Arab at him, with my heart standing still with excitement.

"The deuce!" as I miss him, sticking my spear into the ground, and nearly dislocating my shoulder.

By the time I have wheeled round and recovered my weapon, the pig was leading the others through a low "dâk" jungle of scrub, calculated to push you out of your saddle at every stride. Here he jinked, and No. 4 made a lunge at him, and I was glad to see (and hear) missed him too. Then across a strip of fallow and into a guava orchard over an Irish on-and-off bank. This was a great mistake on my part, for I nearly battered my skull into guava jelly, the branches were so low. I dismounted ignominiously and led out.

When the Arab allowed me to get up again the pig and the party were making for what is, by courtesy, called the island. It is the second preserve surrounded by the Ganges on one side, and on the other, at this time of year only, by low sands and pools. Seeing No. 2 and his horse immersing themselves in one of the latter, as they plunge through after the pig, I decide for what looks like *terra firma*.

But the sands appear more treacherous than the water. Are they quicksands? They yield every now and again alarmingly. Steady, old man! Again one of these queer, soft-looking, deceptive circles. I feel for the master of Ravenswood.

By Jove! in we go, the Arab and I, with a crash, the latter up to his knees, and we part company.

How many broken legs have we between us?

We get up and find ourselves intact.

No. 1 sails by cheerily.

"All right, old chap? 'Ware melon beds! One of the few sources of promotion left in the country!"

Melon beds? Who ever heard of growing melons in a dry river-bed! What a country this India is!

A loud hooroosh from the island. I realise that some-one else has got first spear, and that I have *not* won the Bulampore Cup.

But that evening, when, after a mid-day halt, the final heats have been run off in the twilight, and after dinner we hoist the victor round the mess-tent with psalms and hymns and (very) spiritual songs, I promise myself better luck next time.

IN THE RAJAH'S PALACE.

I MUST confess that I felt very disappointed with her.

I had ridden up to her carriage at the band-stand on the Mall. The strains of the last new waltz out from home were floating among the Millingtonia trees, drowning the champing of the horses' bits, and the chatter of the ayahs and children wandering admiringly round the soldiers.

"Mrs. Ingledene," I had said, "I am getting up an expedition—sport and pic-nicking combined—to the Rajah's palace at Bundelpore, for three days. Will you make one of the party?"

Her face lighted up—such a pretty face—such sweet eyes.

"What a capital idea! I shall be delighted!" she exclaimed. "But—will you mind my bringing a friend—a Mr. Lingmoor, who just then will be staying with us, I think?"

Then it was that I felt disappointed with her.

I had always firmly believed that Jack Ingledene and his wife were devoted to each other. I had only listened with half an ear to Mrs. Crabtree's spiteful stories of the doings at naughty Nynee, during the last season, when the immaculate Mrs. Ingledene was supposed, after the fashion of grass-widows in the hills, to have taken to herself a "bow-wow."

Though Jack Ingledene was on duty on a long court-martial, I knew that he would not object to his wife going with me, an old friend of her father's family, and backed by such an unimpeachable chaperon as Mrs. Crabtree.

But I *was* disappointed when Ethel Ingledene calmly turned up her pretty face to mine, and as good as told me that, unless she was allowed to bring this same "bow-wow," she would not come to my pic-nic.

But all the same, like the old fool I am, with my next breath I expressed how delighted I should be to see Mr. Lingmoor, cursing the Indian "bow-wow" system all the time most devoutly.

As the Collector of Punkahpore, the ruler of a district as large as an English county, and wielding a sway over hundreds of thousands of dusky natives, I am a personage of some importance in the eyes of the neighbouring semi-independent Rajah of Bundelpore. This gentleman, though of dubious character, and unable to write his own name, is the despotic ruler of wide territories, and the happy possessor of diamond aigrettes, such as would delight the heart of an English duchess.

I have standing permission to shoot over his arid plains and rocky hill country, and to stay, whenever I like, in his beautiful summer palace of Bundelpore, which place is but little troubled with his presence, as His Highness prefers his town-house in Guramabad, where he can indulge in European luxuries and vices.

We drove the twenty odd miles which lay between Punkahpore and Bundelpore with relays of horses, along a straight, dusty, tree-bordered road, fairly good as long as it ran in my territory, but execrable as soon as it entered that of the Maharajah. We were a merry party of about a dozen, in three carriages, followed by a camel-carriage, containing the commissariat, the servants, and the rolls of bedding, without which no European travels in India.

I had been somewhat disappointed at my old chum Colonel Tachbrook not turning up. He was retiring, and leaving the country for good, and it was mainly with the object of giving him some good sport that I had arranged the expedition. However, he was delayed up-country, and we were obliged to start without him.

Mrs. Ingledene was looking very pretty and was in the best of spirits. Lionel Lingmoor, a subaltern in the Royal Scilly Islanders, was a good-looking, easy-mannered fellow, whom she appeared to find charming.

The only discordant element was the station doctor, Griffenhoofe, a sneering, ill-natured fellow, who had never forgiven Mrs. Ingledene for snubbing him on her first arrival at Punkahpore, and who chuckled fiendishly over her very open flirtation with Lingmoor.

Bundelpore, built entirely of pale salmon-coloured stone, and gorgeous with carved eaves and mullions, oriel windows, delicate friezes and arches, turrets, cupolas and hanging balconies, lies—a dream of beauty—in the midst of green groves of orange, melon, and mango trees.

On one front a broad stone terrace overlooks the shady garden walks, the ponds, and stone summer-houses; on the other, a large artificial lake, with a little tower and steps at each angle, bathed the very walls of the palace itself.

The Rajah, like many other Indian princes, kept some hunting leopards in a barred cage in the garden, and in the lake some huge black "muggers" or alligators, loathsome-looking beasts, which were fed daily from one of the windows with lumps of flesh.

We drove under the great gate of Bundelpore, saluted by some of the Maharajah's ragamuffin sentries, just as the sun was setting behind some low, bare hills, and flooding the palace with a tint of gold.

The crows were cawing in the trees, ring-doves cooed in the shady depths of the gardens, and flights of tame pigeons circled above the roofs and cupolas. The scene was a delicious change from our painfully uniform bungalows, our straight Mall, and the ceaseless bugle-calls that pervaded Punkahpore.

We dined in a vast hall, with carved Moorish arches, and after dinner we sat about on the terrace, smoking and discussing the plans for the morrow.

I rather fancy I must have had a nap in my easy-chair, for I was aroused by a low, sneering chuckle from Griffenhoofe, sitting next me.

We were alone on the terrace, but the moon, which had just risen, showed us two figures walking down a path in the garden.

"Deuced funny, isn't it? These women are all the same! They come out from England perfect Mimosas, and after a few months' training at a hill-station that's what happens." And he chuckled satirically again.

It was Mrs. Ingledene walking with Lingmoor. The sight made me feel rather sick at heart.

We all turned in early that night, for we were to be up betimes to start in the morning.

The ladies had been installed in the rooms on the left of the great hall, usually allotted to the Rajah's zenana, and we men occupied those on the right. They were not overclean, and rather bare.

I found my servant had laid out my bedding and Griffenhoofe's in one of the top rooms. Opening out of that was another room, where Lingmoor and Colonel Crabtree were to sleep; the other fellows were billeted in the rooms below.

It was a hot night, and Crabtree, who was fussy, said it was less stuffy in one of the verandas, and so departed, leaving Lingmoor in sole possession.

I felt restless and disinclined for sleep. I lay long awake listening to the jackal's screech, the pariah dog's bray, and the lapping of the water of the lake against the wall. I lay watching the bright moonlight throw golden bars across the somewhat dirty walls through the carved glassless window.

Suddenly something roused me. A shadow fell across the moonlight on the wall. The thick curtain in the doorless archway moved aside. A woman's figure entered the room.

There was no mistaking it; it was Ethel Ingledene.

I sprang up, as if to speak to her; but, at that moment, she turned and looked at me. Her face was so unutterably sad that the words froze on my lips.

Then, to my amazement, I saw her push aside the curtain of the doorway leading to the next room, where Lingmoor was sleeping, and disappear behind it.

I sat motionless for a minute or two, for I felt as if someone had dealt me a heavy blow.

Griffenhoofe's voice aroused me; he was awake, too If ever I saw an evil look on a man's face, his wore it at that moment.

"Crabtree was right," he said, gathering up his bedding. "It *will* be much cooler down below."

I followed his example, and departed, but I did not go to sleep.

My thoughts flew back to the happy country-home where I had known Ethel Ingledene as a child with long fair hair—to the good old rector, her father—to honest Jack Ingledene, whom we all liked so much, poor boy! and I felt—well, I felt I should like to have the shooting of Lingmoor. What if, when we were out after deer on the morrow, a shot should chance to go astray! Such things had happened.

But not this time, however. We all shot very straight, and made good bags. I managed to give Lingmoor a wide berth all day, for his good spirits and cheery chaff were even more unbearable to me than Griffenhoofe's unpleasant inuendoes.

It was getting dusk when we returned to the palace. I quite dreaded meeting Mrs. Ingledene, who had not shewn before we started in the morning. Therefore I was very relieved to hear that she had a bad headache from the sun, and would not be able to come down to dinner.

Just as I was having my ante-prandial tub—a simple process, consisting of standing on the bath-room floor, and having pitchers of water poured over one by one's bearer—I heard a familiar voice on the terrace below. It was my old chum, Tachbrook, just arrived. Such a pleasant surprise it was and one which somewhat restored my good humour.

We had a very cheery dinner. Afterwards we amused ourselves throwing bits of meat from a balcony overhanging the lake to the alligators below. The black, slimy monsters rose out of the water into the moonlight, and fought and struggled for the bits we threw, crawling on one another's backs, and opening their huge mouths, set with rows of cruel teeth.

Miss Crabtree, the spinster of our party, turned away with a shudder.

"It gives me the creeps to look at them," she said. "I want to talk of something more pleasant—your charming friend, Colonel Tachbrook. What a dear old thing he is! Now, tell me, is it true what I hear, that there is some romantic story about him—that he was engaged to a girl who was killed in the Mutiny, and that that's the reason he was never married? Do tell me!"

Of course I had heard something of the kind about Tachbrook, but I was not going to divulge any secret of my friend's.

"My dear young lady," I replied, mysteriously, "you are as curious and as romantic as all your sex. Pray, believe it if you like."

"You are very irritating," she laughed, and turned away!

Then Tachbrook himself came up.

"This Bundelpore Rajah of yours, wasn't he very troublesome to us in '57?" he asked.

"It was his father, not the present man. He turned against us from the first, don't you remember, and attacked and killed the Europeans at Guramabad, and at Punkahpore."

A shadow crossed Tachbrook's face. To hide it, he caressed his gray moustache pensively.

"I was away before Delhi then. But I remember it all now—I remember it all."

He turned aside, and changed the conversation.

Griffenhoofe had given up his place in my sleeping apartment to Tachbrook, much to my delight. I was dog-tired, and trusted that I should be undisturbed by any such unpleasant episode as that of the night before. But Tachbrook appeared restless, and not inclined to sleep.

"Rum thing it is, old man, I should be stopping in one of Bundelpore's palaces. You've heard me speak of Ethel Brooke sometimes—that dear little girl I was engaged to in '57, before the troubles began. She went away to stay with some people at Guramabad just before the Mutiny broke out. I was ordered suddenly to Delhi, and then came the Guramabad massacre. I never heard of her again—not a sign—not a word. Thank God, the Rajah died the death he deserved—done to death by a traitor! And now his son is our good friend, and I am his guest! Such is life! Heigh ho!"

He lighted a cigar, and smoked me to sleep.

How long I slept I don't know. A sudden cry from Tachbrook woke me with a start.

"Ethel! Great God! it is Ethel!"

I sprang up, and there, stealing in through the curtain, exactly as she had done the night before, came Mrs. Ingledene.

Tachbrook stared at her like a madman.

"Poor fellow!" I said to myself. "These sad memories have upset his head."

She glided behind the curtain into Lingmoor's room. Tachbrook jumped up, and followed her.

"At any price, a scandal must be prevented," thought I, and I sprang up, too, and followed him.

Lingmoor was sleeping the sleep of youth, and of a hard day's shooting.

Tachbrook, with outstretched arms, stared at the dark form, which slowly flitted across the room.

She passed through the open window, out on to the balcony overhanging the lake.

A horrible fear seized me. She saw herself discovered, and would not live to face the shame.

"Stop her! stop her!" I cried.

We both rushed out on to the balcony.

It was empty.

C., M. G.

The night breeze ruffled the dark surface of the lake in the depths of which the muggers were sleeping.

Tachbrook and I glared at each other, too horrified to speak.

Then a voice called me from the stairs.

"You are wanted at once, Collector Sahib. There is an old crone, the mother, or aunt, or some such relation of the Rajah, who lives in a little house in the garden, and who is dying, and wants to see you very urgently."

"Oh! do come," said another voice, a very sweet one. "I did what I could for her this afternoon when you were away, and I found her so ill. But she has something on her mind to tell you, and I promised you should come. Be quick, or it will be too late!"

The speaker was Mrs. Ingledene, standing at the door of my room, looking lovely in a white peignoir. At first I thought she was a ghost. But I grasped her arm. It was firm flesh and blood.

"I will go at once," I said. "You go back to bed."

As I went down the stairs, I heard Lingmoor's voice calling:

"Send some one with brandy. Colonel Tachbrook has fainted."

They led me to one of those little garden-houses, common in the east, where an almost sightless, toothless old hag lay at her last gasp.

"You are the Government's servant," she said, " the great sahib—you are good to my nephew, the Maharajah —you have forgiven of your great clemency the wickedness of my brother, when he killed your people, your women and children. I have something to say before I die, if your Highness will listen."

She spoke with difficulty, and in gasps. I bent down to catch her words.

"Her spirit came to me to-day, so I know that I am dying—the spirit of the beautiful young white maiden, with the yellow hair, whom my brother carried off from Guramabad, when he killed the rest, and whom he brought here. She was kind to me, the spirit; she has forgiven me. For I took her jewels. I have them now. I wish to give them back to a white sahib, lest the devils should torment me when I am gone. The Rajah shut her up in the top rooms—no one could hear her cries there—she could not escape—he put men on the stairs to keep the door. He delighted in the yellow-haired maiden—he would have made her his favourite wife—but one morning, when we opened the door—she was gone. Her jewels were there—and a little holy book she carried in her bosom—see, here they are."

From under her pillow she drew, with feeble grasp, a yellow, worn, little English prayer-book, and a gold brooch and earrings, and gave them to me.

As I opened the book I was aware of two people looking over my shoulder. Tachbrook and Mrs. Ingledene had followed me.

The fly-leaf was yellow and dirty, but the name on it perfectly legible—

"ETHEL BROOKE, September, 1856,
"Hardleigh Hall."

A great groan broke from Tachbrook.

"It is her name—her writing," he answered, and hid his face in his hands.

"That was my mother's sister's name," gasped Mrs. Ingledene. "Their home was at Hardleigh Hall—I remember hearing she came out to India, and was killed in——"

Tachbrook interrupted her.

"You are her niece?" he asked, in a gentle voice. "You are her very image; I think I see her again."

And he drew her to him, and kissed her on the forehead.

I turned over the gold brooch in my hand.

"There is a miniature in the back, see!"

Mrs. Ingledene looked, and gave a cry.

"That is my mother when a girl. I know it quite well—I have one like it!"

There was a faint gurgle from the bed. The old native woman in the corner, who had been watching us, fell back dead.

We left her, and passed out into the cool garden, where the bird-life was just awaking.

Mrs. Ingledene disappeared to her own apartment. Tachbrook went out alone for a walk. I thought it best to leave him to himself. We were great friends, but after a discovery such as this, not even the greatest friends can be any comfort.

Worn out by the night's emotions, I fell asleep till breakfast time. When I joined the rest of the party in the great hall, I found everyone devouring letters and papers just brought out from Punkahpore by a messenger.

Mrs. Ingledene rushed at me with outstretched hands:

"I want you to be the first to hear, for you are my oldest friend in this country, and I have so hated to have a secret from you! Listen, I have just got my home letters, and papa has, at last, given his consent to Nellie's marriage with Lionel Lingmoor. I'm so happy! You remember Nellie, the youngest of us all—they got engaged when he was home last summer on leave—and papa was furious. So they have been corresponding through me, and I have been doing all I can to help them. And now that Lionel is to get his captaincy, papa has given in. I'm so glad, for he's such a nice fellow, isn't he? though, of course, I shall never think anyone quite good enough for Nell!"

"I remember Nell perfectly. I carried her pick-a-back the last time I saw her. And as I can't congratulate her personally, let me do it by proxy, dear little lady."

So saying, I bent down and kissed Mrs. Ingledene on the forehead. If Jack could have read in my heart how penitent I was for my horrible suspicions, I do not think he would have objected.

Just then Crabtree bustled up.

"Here's Lingmoor been getting into such a mess—just like a griff. He's gone and shot one of the Rajah's muggers—didn't think there was any harm. Come and see what's to be done!"

"Nothing, I should think, except to administer a few judicious rupees all round, to keep it quiet," I replied, and followed Crabtree to the steps leading down to the lake, where Lingmoor was surveying the huge carcase of the dead alligator.

"'Pon my honour, I didn't realize they were preserved! I'm awfully sorry."

"You may as well have him stuffed now you've got him," I remarked. "He's a splendid fellow, the grandfather of them all, I should judge."

I called a low-caste native, who began to cut up the animal.

Presently, in his stomach, we came on something small and glittering. I picked it up. It was a gold ring.

I rubbed it bright, and then saw some letters engraved on the inside:

"Ethel, from W. T.," I read aloud.

"Will you let me have it?" said a voice behind me.

And I handed it to Tachbrook without a word.

TWO STRINGS.

AT home, in the Park in England, it was white waistcoat weather, when women appear in sweet cotton frocks, when the social air buzzes with cricket and yachting talk, and men begin to feel their gout and to say they must go to Hamburg. Up in the Himalayas, where the little collection of châlets dotted about the precipices among the ilex and the rhododendrons form what is called a hill-station, the monsoon was at its height. Drip, drip, drip—hammer, hammer, hammer—for sometimes a day and a night at a stretch, down upon the corrugated iron roofs of the bungalows, came the rain. The frogs and the leeches, the fungi and the ferns, grew and multiplied, but it was enough to damp the cheeriest, giddiest nature that ever revelled in the ceaseless round of frivolity and fooling that goes on at Murree.

Ten o'clock at night. A wood fire made of damp logs that declined to burn brightly. The wind howling among the deodars, the rain pelting, the shivering servants rolled up in rugs asleep in their own log huts— not a soul stirring in the draughty little bungalow but herself. It was most depressing; the kind of evening when every worry, every error, everything you would rather not have said, assumes magnified proportions and haunts you.

So it was with Queenie Vayle, though a more unlikely looking subject for the horrors of remorse and depression did not exist. Such golden hair—the true dark gold colour, such appealing brown eyes, and a nose just the least bit *retroussé* to give piquancy to the face, and only one-and-twenty.

They had considered themselves engaged ever since Queenie was in short frocks with a pigtail of gold-brown hair; and the hideous uniform of the Royal Military College, Sandhurst, did its best, though unsuccessfully, to take off from Reggy Vayle's good looks and well-set-up, manly figure. Then, in order to prevent the possibility of their ever changing their minds or coming across any one they liked better than themselves, they were married at the end of Queenie's first season, and prepared to make the acquaintance of the world together. It was tempting the gods, and the usual result followed.

Two years later Vayle's regiment was ordered to India. Queenie's baby died—the young mother and the ayah together muddled it to death; she got fever, and the doctor packed her off to the hills. Reggy could get no leave.

To the Mayo Hotel at Simree that season, sent up to recover himself in the cool from a polo accident, lame and interesting, came Cis Lorrimer, the ugliest fellow in the Crimson Cuirassiers, and the most popular and the most fascinating. He found himself sitting at the *table d'hôte* next Mrs. Vayle, and he forthwith took her under his charge. She was so new to India, to life in general, and such a refreshing change from most of Cis's female friends. Queenie's silly little head was soon perfectly turned by the attentions of a hero such as she had never met before; a man who, when his foot was upon his native Piccadilly, was one of a set royalty affected, and whose every nod and word was accepted with effusion by the *élite* of Simree society. In India, where the table of precedence is ruled by the number of rupees drawn, a little flavour of real aristocracy goes a long way.

Under the influence of Lorrimer, Queenie Vayle developed wonderfully. She had come to Simree a simple child; before many weeks were out she was a woman—and a woman devoured with the great passion of her life. The glamour of Lorrimer was over her; Reggy became more and more commonplace and uninteresting, because so familiar; her letters to him fewer and fewer.

At last, however, he got one, the penning of which was, of all the foolish things Queenie had done in her silly little life, the most foolish. She wrote and told him that she found she no longer loved him as real love goes; but, having met the one man in the world for her, she was off on a trip into Cashmere with him. She was very sorry, but she couldn't help it, and hoped he would forgive her; or words to that effect.

Reggy Vayle—an honest, straightforward, and very young Englishman, grilling away at Punkahpore—did not prove of the ordinary type of patient, acquiescent Anglo-Indian husband, who calls his wife's "bow-wow" by his Christian name, and takes care to give a few days' notice before he runs up to the hill-station on leave.

There was a fearful scandal. Society in India winks at a good deal, but the law makes up for it by severity. The Cashmere trip had to be cut short; the case came on in the High Court; and Cis Lorrimer had to sacrifice everything and make a bolt of it to somewhere—Japan or Australia. The court gave him two years and mulcted him handsomely. He was absent without leave, and, after the usual interval, the *Gazette* recorded that her Majesty had no further need of his services.

* * * *

And now another monsoon had come round again, and Queenie Vayle sat solitary, listening to the rain, utterly alone in the world. Lorrimer made no sign, and her family at home had cast her off as completely as her husband. She felt so utterly wretched that she would have given anything for a kind word from any one. But women looked askance at her, for in India great importance is attached to the new commandment —thou shalt not be found out; and as to kind words from men, well, it hadn't quite come to that yet, though it might soon, Queenie felt. For life was intolerable.

It was well-nigh intolerable to some one else, too— a man who had arrived that day from the plains and was going on to-morrow into Cashmere after big game. Reggy Vayle felt in the thoroughly British mood for killing something. He could not kill Lorrimer, for he did not know where he was to be found. So he was going to kill ibex.

It was a mere chance that in the hotel reading-room he saw Queenie's name in the visitors' list. He had no idea she was up at Murree, and the shock of the surprise gave him the oddest impulse. The memory of Queenie rose up before him as she had been a year before—pure, lovely, his own; and a great hunger came over the man just to see her once more, not to speak to her, not even to let her know he saw her—only to see her for the last time.

In the dark verandah of Queenie's little bungalow stood a tall figure, the rain running off his mackintosh in streams, on to the flooring. There was a chink between the curtains, and, by pressing his face against the pane, he could see her distinctly. The gleam of the lamp caught her golden head, as she sat, with hands clasped on her knee, gazing into the fire, looking utterly dejected, a lonely little figure. A great feeling of pity and remorse stole over Reggy. She looked so young; he had sworn to love and to cherish her. Instinctively he stretched out his arms towards her, when——

A sepulchral cough sounded from the corner of the verandah. It was the watchman, the *chokedar*, who is supposed to guard each bungalow at night, rousing in his slumber and announcing his alertness. Reggy had no choice but to fly precipitately.

Indian postal officials are crassness itself. Vayle's servant had been to inquire for his master's letters as soon as the latter had arrived at Murree, and they were lying on the table in his room when he returned from his Enoch Arden visit. He opened them mechanically. One began " My own darling Queenie," and was signed

"Yours, as ever, Cecil Lorrimer." The address on the envelope was *Mrs.* Vayle, but neither the post-office people nor Vayle himself had noticed it. A cheque for a large sum fell from its folds.

It was a good letter, and showed the writer in a better light than he had appeared in before. All being lost for both of them—for Queenie, home and fame; for him, his position in the world, in the dear old corps—Lorrimer, who had been getting his affairs straight, wrote to ask her to come out at once to Tasmania to marry him and start life afresh. It was a straightforward kind of letter, and it was more. It was a love-letter. Queenie had not been to him merely a toy, to be played with and cast aside.

Vayle sat with the letter in his hand going through a great fight with himself. He had imagined that Queenie was utterly dead to him; that he had cast her off for ever. But now, with this other man's offer lying before him, a queer feeling of jealousy came over him. He saw her again as he had just seen her—lonely, sad, desolate. He remembered her in the old years; his little wife, she had called herself, ever since she was in her teens. All her treachery was forgotten; he felt he could not let her go.

Lorrimer's letter fluttered into the fire and curled to ashes among the logs.

Ten minutes later Queenie starts at the sound of an opening door. All the windows are doors in India, and none are ever locked. She turns and shrieks, for a man stands in the verandah with a passionate look on his face.

He is kneeling before her; his hands clutch hers convulsively. For she looks to him just the same as she did that Christmas when she blushed and told him she was getting too big to be kissed under the mistletoe —just the same as she did in her bridal veil in the village church at home.

"Darling!" he pleads hoarsely, "darling! will you forgive me? Will you come back to me?"

Far away in Tasmania the other one, waiting and longing, is not in it. It seems so natural to rest her head on Reggy's shoulder, and there lay down the weary load of care and desolation which oppressed her, and shut out for ever the hideous nightmare of the last few months; and they are remarried within a few days.

* * * *

The scene changes to the Park and white-waistcoat weather. Cis Lorrimer, landed at Charing Cross that morning, stands in a quiet corner under the trees, with his hat tilted over his eyes, and sees ghosts. Ghosts of the men and women he has known in town before the Crimsons sailed for India five years ago. Men grown stout, women gone off; men grown bald, women with unmistakably increased hair. Frocks new and wonderful; a new curve in a hat brim. Familiar forms; strange faces. But there, flitting down, chatting gaily to nice-looking women, a well-remembered face with golden hair, but looking happier, more peaceful, than when he saw it last.

He watches her across the Row and put into a hansom at the corner by her friends. Then he jumps into another and follows it to Gargantuan Mansions.

That evening, when the sunlight, darkened by the awning over the balcony, casts deep shadows in the little drawing-room of the flat, Queenie Vayle sits alone, toying with her tea.

There is an electric ring, a footstep in the tiny passage, and a voice—well remembered—speaking, makes Queenie start to her feet.

The maid, without a word, is showing some one into the dim room. Hands are held out towards her.

"Queenie! Queenie! at last I have found you!"

She gives a low cry of pain and half turns away.

"Won't you speak to me? You never answered. Speak to me now; do, Queenie. I'm doing well; a different fellow; and—and—I want you, Queenie."

She looks up at him for a few moments, and then a light breaks upon her.

She motions him away.

"You mustn't speak like that, Cis. It can't be! It is all over!"

His face grows hard and set suddenly, as if he had been struck a blow.

"What do you mean, Queenie? Has anyone come between us? Good God!"

She moves to the door that divides the drawing-room from the little dining-room and opens it very softly.

There is an odour of tobacco about the room, and Reggy Vayle lies back in an arm-chair enjoying an ante-prandial nap and snoring slightly.

"Yes," she says, pointing to him, "some one has—my husband!"

She crosses the room on tiptoe and, bending her fair head over the back of his chair, kisses him lightly on the forehead.

When she goes back to the drawing-room it is empty.

* * * * *

Everyone knows how Cis Lorrimer, late of the Crimson Cuirassiers, got into the Mounted Infantry in Egypt and was killed at the Ghazi Dhru Wells business.

A MODERN LOCHINVAR.

Mrs. Splatter was the biggest lady in the Anglo-Indian station of Noluck. I am not, of course, alluding to her corporeal size, though that too was worthy of note, but to her social position. She was, to use the native term applied to her and her ilk, the "burra mem," or big woman.

What matter that the progenitors of her lesser half ("my husband, the Commissioner," as she was always careful to designate him) were not unconnected with a hosiery shop in St. James's Street, and that her own parents owned a crockery establishment in the Strand? In Noluck, East Indies, such are the stern rules of official precedence, Mrs. Splatter went into dinner before everybody else.

Mr. Commissioner Splatter was a man of a mosaic temperament, and, though he ruled hundreds of thousands of her Imperial Majesty's dusky subjects, scattered over an area as large as an English county, Mrs. Splatter governed him.

The eldest child of the Splatter pair was Ella, a winsome little person of seventeen. She had just "come out" (in India girls do indeed come out) per steamship *Honolulu*, like European goods, to enliven the somewhat severe commissionorial residence, a huge, whitewashed, double-storied bungalow, shut in with verandahs so as to render the windows almost invisible, and standing in a square yard, yclept a garden, and fringed with the mud huts of the tribe of red-coated retainers who loafed on the broad flight of steps.

Ella "took after" her papa, as the nurses say. She had no very decided opinions or characteristics—an excellent thing, both in a young lady and in a senior member of the Civil Service. But it was certinly from neither parent that she got her fresh English beauty and cheery girlish ways.

Ella had been conveyed to India under the unimpeachable chaperonage of Mrs. Lynx, whose husband was civil surgeon at Noluck, and to whose care Mrs. Splatter unhesitatingly entrusted her daughter. But the best-laid plans of mice and mothers often deviate from the straight line, and certainly Mrs. Splatter had not foreseen that, owing to Mrs. Lynx being laid on her back with a sprained ankle for the greater part of the voyage, Miss Ella would be free to make and to cultivate pretty extensively the fascinating acquaintance of Lieutenant George Eston, of the 130th Foot, without a penny beyond his pay. How he allowed pretty Ella to leave the ship without proposing to her might well be a puzzle to any man who had looked into her blue eyes. But probably young Bridges, the engineer, had something to do with it. He was perpetually coming up and flushing the couple when Eston, in a cosy corner, was about to say something irretrievable.

In the short twilight of a spring evening (Indian days are much of a muchness as regards length, and the blind man's holiday is short), Mrs. Splatter sat in the reading-room of the Noluck Club, laying down the law to a representative gathering of Noluck female society. The Chutter Munzil (profanely dubbed the Chatter Munzil) is a decayed royal palace of stucco on the evil-smelling banks of a torpid river. Like most Indian clubs, it has one room thrown open to ladies, where they may peruse the *Queen* and the picture papers, and discuss the far more absorbing topics of local scandal and domestic grievances.

Outside on the terrace a long line of patient carriages awaited their mistresses and masters. The grooms were mostly engaged in lighting the lamps as the darkness fell, while from the club came a click of billiard-balls and a popping of corks.

Weary of the endless stories of the frisky ways of Mrs. Frayle, or of the impertinence of Mrs. Paynter, the wife of the colonel of the Lancer regiment quartered in the cantonments, or of the peculations of cooks, and tired of papers three weeks' old, the bloom of whose contents had been rubbed off by telegrams, Ella left her mother and Mrs. Colonel de Ferret deep in confab, and strayed on to the steps outside the open French windows. The tom-toms and cow-horns which had beaten to evening prayers were hushed in the teeming native city, and a subtle odour of objectionable smoke crept over the land, and announced that the mild Hindoo was cooking his evening meal. Suddenly the four-in-hand brake of the Lancers drove up on to the terrace with a dash, and a bevy of white-breeched and booted and spurred polo players hied them into the club.

But one came along to the reading-room and peeped in cautiously. After looking round the group of ladies he turned away, and in so doing brushed against Ella in the darkness.

"Beg your pardon, I'm sure," he murmured, raising his cap.

Ella started and hesitated a minute. It was so dark that she might be mistaken in the voice. Then she made a bold shot.

"Good evening, Mr. Eston," and in another minute they were telling all the news they had bottled up for each other since they had parted at Bombay. What an age it seemed! Yet it was only a month ago.

They had not half finished when it grew raw and cold on the riverside, and Mrs. Splatter was heard within, about to depart, and beginning her last words.

"I must fly—there's mamma coming!" whispered Ella. "When shall I see you again?"

"When you like," answered he.

"Oh! not till then?" she replied, with a bewitching smile, which betrayed her ironical tone, and took shelter under her mother's wing.

With great presence of mind Eston advanced and called up the carriage. The open landau drew up, driven by a native coachman in a dark tunic over his skin-tight white-cotton trousers, and who held the reins on a level with his nose. Two grooms, dressed to match him, clung on to the back of the carriage, armed with yâk-tail fly-whisks, and rushed to open the door. Eston helped the ladies in, and Mrs. Splatter, who mistook him in the dark for someone else, was very affable.

"Who is that young man?" inquired the lady, as they rumbled off to the Civil Lines. "I thought at first it was Mr. Cramwell." (Mr. Cramwell was the unmarried joint-magistrate.)

But when Ella explained that it was only a common or garden subaltern, whom she had met on board ship, and who was staying with a friend in the 131st in cantonments, Mrs. Splatter sniffed scornfully. In virtue of her exalted position as the wife of one of the "senior" heaven-born, Mrs. Splatter abhorred what she termed the military. A rising young civil servant, worth three hundred a year dead or alive, was of more value in her sight than many soldiers with curled moustaches and bravery of gold lace and spurs. She gave Ella forthwith to understand as much, and the latter's spirits, which had risen so ridiculously at the unexpected rencontre with Eston, promptly sank to zero.

Next morning, at the orthodox calling hour, between twelve and two, Mr. Eston sent in his card for Mrs. Splatter by one of the red-coated retainers on the steps. Then he followed it into the large drawing-room, furnished with real English upholstered tables and sofas. But the great lady was distinctly frigid, and other callers, of more importance than a subaltern, engrossed her attention. Poor Eston hardly got in a few words alone to Ella, before a further batch of visitors caused him to beat a precipitate retreat.

Nevertheless, something must have been arranged between them, for next day he joined Ella in her morning ride up the shady Mall, and they had a gallop together round the racecourse, the only soft going in all Noluck, and that a littered course. Ella looked pretty even under her hideous white sun-helmet, and Eston blessed the Indian custom by which grooms pursue their mistresses on foot only. Of course, as they were going to ride at a good pace, it was only humane to dispense with the services of the white-robed attendant and bid him await their return.

No doubt it was exceedingly wrong of Ella to be riding about alone thus with a decided detrimental, all unbeknown to her mother, while the latter was occupied with domestic cares, such as giving out the stores checking the cook's accounts, and counting over the dirty dusters. But in the first place, even had Mrs. Splatter been able to chaperone her daughter on horseback, she would, indeed, have needed a weight-carrier; and, in the second, the Anglo-Indian system of bringing up children away from their parents is hardly conducive to much sympathy and confidence, and Mrs. Splatter was hardly the mother to elicit much of the latter.

Eston had only ten days' leave, and he was not the man to let the grass grow under his feet. About 6-30 A.M. one deliciously fresh morning (the days were growing perceptibly hotter), all among the glowing bouganvillias and alamandas of the fort gardens, haunted with sad memories of British heroism, he told Ella what she had guessed already, the while sapient crows croaked at them from the mango branches, and shrill green parrots jeered at them as they shrieked past like a streak of green lightning. But the doves cooed to them sympathetically from the peepul-trees.

But, alas for the course of true love! The upstart of that sweet morning's compact was a stormy interview between Ella and her mother, which sent the latter to bed with a headache and tears.

When Eston arrived at noon to see the commissioner, he was met by the stern remark that, in Anglo-Indian parlance, the door was shut, and in the evening Mrs. Splatter and Ella cut him dead as they passed him on the Mall in their afternoon drive. He noticed Ella's eyes were red.

Next day was Sunday, and the last day of Eston's leave. In accordance with the convenient Indian custom that runs all the expresses at night, and so materially lengthens one's existence, Eston was to rejoin his regiment by that evening's mail train. But he felt he could not leave without seeing Ella once more. So he did a thing he could never remember doing except when with the regiment and on duty since he left Harrow, and that was—going to church.

He was rewarded, Ella sat in the front seat, the commissioner's. Eston secured one at right-angles to her, and thus turned Mrs. Splatter's flank. But when one is a "burra mem," and sits in the uppermost seats in the synagogue, one must be very devout. So the latter lady missed a great deal of the eye telegraphy which went on between the lovers all service time.

The weather was getting hot; white-frilled punkahs were swaying methodically, pulled by heathen in the verandah, over a congregation consisting of a sprinkling of black-coated civilians and their families, a fringe of whitey-brown clerks and shopkeepers, and a brilliant patch of soldiers in divers uniforms, who had marched to the very church doors with their bands playing joyous melodies. These infantry, as usual, ever since the outbreak of the Mutiny at Meerut while the troops were in church, had each man his rifle resting in the book-shelf before him. Even the chaplain fanned himself languidly as he began a long-winded discourse which, combined with the punkahs and the early hour (church began at 8 A.M. now), soon sent Eston off into a half-waking dream, not unconnected with a church in which Ella played a prominent part. So sleepy was he that when, at the conclusion of the service, the soldier who did verger came round with the alms-bag and offered him one of those little tickets whereon is to be inscribed the amount of the donation—as no one carries any coin in India—Eston clean forgot where he was, and, hastily snatching the proffered pencil, wrote quickly, with hazy recollections of the club:—

"One whisky and soda. G. Eston, Lieut., 130th."

Shortly after Eston's departure Mrs. Splatter carried off Ella to the neighbouring hill-station of Simree for the hot-weather months. Old Splatter remained behind at work, enjoying his whist and billiards at the club, as he never got enough of them when under conjugal surveillance.

Cramwell, too, the rising young civilian, was off to the hills. The fickle goddess of promotion had marked him for her own. He was caught up into the seventh heaven of the Local Government, and Noluck hot weathers would know him no more. *En revanche*, Rose Cottage, the little châlet wherein Mrs. Splatter had planted herself among the rhododendrons, became very familiar with his presence, and his attentions to Ella became daily more marked. Mrs. Splatter smiled upon his suit, and probably no one would have had any objections to make to the affair, if Cramwell had not been an out-and-out red-haired cad of the first water, probably "riz" in a Scotch grammar school and with no manners whatever, while Ella was quite the prettiest girl that season at Simree.

By way of setting in motion the mill-wheel round of gaieties which engross the frivolous mind of the mountain Capua, the august hostess of Government House issued invitations for a fancy ball on the Queen's Birthday. Forthwith the feminine mind became much exercised as to costumes, and in every verandah sat a cross-legged native tailor, stitching away at fancy dresses, which he held with his toes. It was to be a tremendous function, and rumour even whispered that Mrs. General Money, the best-dressed woman in Simree, had telegraphed to Paris for a dress to eclipse every one else's.

In the midst of all this excitement, who should turn up at the Empire Hotel, a few days before the ball but George Eston. Regardless of the envenomed glance shot at him by Mrs. Splatter when he ran against her in the Assembly Rooms at an afternoon concert, he went off straightway to Messrs. Sharpe and Dunn, the English tailors. From among the chaos on their workroom floor he had picked out for him Mr. Cramwell's fancy dress, and immediately ordered for himself the exact counterpart, bribing Messrs. S. and D. to solemn secrecy.

Mr. Cramwell, after much cogitation, had decided to disguise his red head in the grey locks and venerable beard of a monk, while a flowing black robe, girt with a hempen cord, was to veil his manly form. George Eston did exactly the same; and when the Simree world found themselves—a motley crew—assembled under the gubernatorial chandeliers, there was not a pin to choose between the two monks. In fact, every one imagined that it was one and the same ascetic prowling about in two places at once, except a few who, as the evening wore on, imagined they saw double. No one was more taken in than Mrs. Splatter, whose argus eye was continually spying her daughter sitting out in dim corners with the unsaintly anchorite, and who gloated over the sight.

She was jubilant, indeed, when at the close of the entertainment her six panting bearers deposited her in her "jampan" in the verandah of Rose Cottage. The Lieutenant-Governor's supper had been excellent, and to it she had done ample justice. True, that a "seniorer" lady than herself had been taken in by the Great Panjandrum himself to the solemn, sit-down, square meal which is such an important feature in an Indian ball; but he had honoured Mrs. Splatter with a quadrille. So she turned to Ella effusively :—

"Well, my dear, and how have you enjoyed yourself?"

"Awfully, mamma!"

"And how did you get on with—with him? Did he say anything, Ella?"

Ella's long lashes drooped over her eyes, and her very neck and shoulders blushed.

"Well—yes—mamma."

"Dear child! I am pleased! But I won't bother you at this time of night. Go and get some beauty sleep, and tell me everything in the morning."

Ella turned away hanging her head. But at the door of her room she came back again.

"Mamma, won't you kiss me?"

Mrs. Splatter folded her to her capacious bosom.

But next morning, while the "burra mem" was still wrapped in slumber, dreaming sweet dreams of *pâté de foie gras* and a seat on the Legislative Council for her lesser half, a tonga might have been seen whirling away down the road to the plains as fast as a pair of galloping ponies could draw it. Under the hood, on the back seat, sat Eston and Ella.

The sun rose brilliantly from behind the forest-clad mountains, as they tore down the zigzags, round sharp curves, above overhanging precipices, through deep gorges. Torrents roared unseen in the ravines, and waterfalls answered them from the crags above. The koel boomed its cuckoo-like note across the valley, and cowbells tinkled from upland pastures. Patches of rosy rhododendrons dyed the hill-sides crimson. At the sound of the blast of the coachman's horn, long trains of heavily laden bullock-wagons crept out of the way of the clattering tonga, which a fresh pair of ponies every five miles carried farther and farther away from parental ire.

Little Mrs. Grey, the wife of a captain in Eston's regiment, sat in the evening of that day in her verandah trying to feel cool after her evening drive in the furnace-like atmosphere of Guramghur. Of course she might have been away amusing herself in the hills, but her Charley could not get leave, and so, as she put it, she meant to "stick it out" with him. Great was her surprise to see a station gharry drive up, from which emerged Eston.

"I thought you were up at Simree?" was her greeting.

"So I was. Mrs. Grey, will you do something for me?"

He led her into the drawing-room, with such an unusual expression of triumphant anxiety blended on his face that Mrs. Grey asked herself if he had either come to grief in some way, or been made A.D.C. up at Simree. But Eston was a great friend of the Greys, and in his need he had not counted on them in vain. After a very short explanation, the little woman ran down the steps and, opening the carriage-door, helped Ella out. The latter, after a minute's hesitation, flung herself into Mrs. Grey's arms, and Mrs. Grey kissed the sweet little face, where the smiles struggled with the tears.

"And now," remarked Eston, when this eminently feminine performance was concluded, "I'm off to see the padre."

They were married next morning in the whitewashed barn which did duty for a church at Guramghur—married quite early, while yet the barracks were astir with the usual matutinal bustle and noisy with bugle-calls, while people were going for the before-breakfast rides, and ere the morning mail-train sauntered into Guramghur station.

In it came Mr. and Mrs. Splatter, the former armed with a thick stick, and the latter, woman-like, with her daughter's clothes. But they came too late. When they entered the Greys' breakfast-room, Ella was Mrs. Eston.

After a preliminary outburst every one decided to make the best of everything, and Splatter *père et mère* returned next day to Simree, without their daughter, bearing with them a grain of comfort in the knowledge that, though their son-in-law might be penniless, yet he was the nephew of a real baronet. The thought of her child's uncle-in-law somewhat consoled Mrs. Splatter when, later on in the season, Cramwell became engaged to the decidedly plain daughter of her great rival the Commissioneress of Todiabad. At any rate, it gave her something to enlarge upon, when the latter lady condoled with her in such an irritating manner.

But through the scorching hot weather and the drenching monsoon which followed, Ella never grumbled over her dinner of herbs in the little thatched bungalow, or sighed for the stalled ox and the luxury of a thermantidote in the Commissioner's mansion at Noluck. What matters it if a subaltern's pay does not go far? Are not the banks of India a refuge for the destitute? And little reck young lovers of heavy interest and a day of reckoning. What matters the lively mosquito, the maddening prickly heat, the thermometer at ninety-something, or the rains coming down and making life one long Turkish bath, or coming through and necessitating an umbrella in bed, while reptiles and insects find a happy home in the room? Certainly the rainy season in the plains is hardly a joyous one, and yet Ella and Eston were ridiculously happy.

But with the clearer skies of returning sunshine of September a vague dread spread through Guramghur. The cholera-fiend hovered over the native city, and struck down his victims in the crowded gaol and the busy bazaar. He stretched his sword over cantonments, and the troops fled before him into cholera-camp, with their bands playing, it is true, but leaving some of their number behind them in hospital.

He spared not the Estons' little thatched bungalow. Thence, one evening, all that was mortal of Ella was borne on a gun-carriage down the Mall, along which she had cantered so gaily only the day before, and laid to rest in the little white-walled cemetery, crowded with nameless soldiers' graves and thick with children's mounds.

MY FIRST SNIPE.

"THEY'RE in, old man! I'll be hanged if they're not!"

This was Captain Cartridge's remark to Shotwell, and puzzled me somewhat, as I lay half asleep in a long lounging chair in the ante-room, with my feet raised higher than my head on the broad elongated arms.

What were in, I asked myself, sleepily. It could not be the letters, for it was yesterday that I had received Messrs. Lappel and Son's polite and patient "to account rendered," from far away Bond-street. It could not be charming Mrs. Dashington and her pretty sister, the only women worth speaking to in the station, for everyone knew that Shotwell and Cartridge had a soul above paying calls.

Only a month before H.M. troopship *Alligator* had disgorged me at Bombay, and my evil star and the Great Indian Peninsula Railway had led me to join my regiment at the small and remote station of Guramghur. Talk of a one-horse place: Guramghur was only a one-pony place, for we were but a poor infantry corps without the wherewithal to spend on polo or pig-sticking, or even paper-chasing; and one "tat" wherewith to canter to and from mess, and to drive in our bamboo carts, satisfied our modest aspirations. We wanted but little in the way of horseflesh at Guramghur, but, in the case of Colonel Cormorant, who weighed over sixteen stone, we wanted that little strong. No, there was nothing to recommend Guramghur—no society, very little work, as we were the only troops, and but for the society of the Dashingtons, I must have been bored to death. But this is a digression.

Inquiry on my part elicited the information from Shotwell that it was the snipe that formed the topic of their conversation. How dense of me! As if when Shotwell and Cartridge got together they ever talked of anything else but killing something. All the same, we were proud of our two crack shots, for I fear we were rather a "dog and walking-stick" regiment, and we would descant on their wonderful bags to other non-sporting characters.

Shotwell added, kindly: "You should go out and have a try at the snipe, my boy; finest sport out!"

My ambition was fired. So they had arrived, these mysterious birds of passage, winging their way from far northern steppes over pathless snows, to alight for a few days in some quiet morass on monotonous Indian levels, ere they sped on again, no one knows whither. Did I not possess a brand new gun that had never yet left its case? I would sally forth and deal death and destruction among the snipe, and astonish Mrs. Dashington by sending her in a dish of them for dinner.

Returning to my bungalow I ordered my bearer to bring before me some trustworthy "shikari" who would lead my infant footsteps in the way in which they should go—after snipe. He arrived, and except that he was a trifle less clothed and more unkempt than the usual run of natives, there was nothing to denote especial woodcraft about him. After a three-cornered conversation between the "shikari," the bearer, and myself, and a prodigious amount of misunderstanding, it was arranged that on the morrow I was to shoot the Paniput Jheel, where the snipe were as thick as mosquitoes.

It was dawn when my bearer succeeded in the, to him, dangerous task of waking me. The air was chill, with the welcome and delicious crispness of the cold weather. No one seemed astir except the crows, who cawed monotonously in the branches, and even the "chokedar," or private watchman—the ostensible protector of our lives and property—was still asleep in a corner of the verandah. In the shafts of the cart standing by the steps was the "slave," a most useful grey pony, with no particular faults except that of an inveterate habit of jibbing at starting, and of such a vicious temper that no one except his own "syce" could approach within two yards of him in the stable. After the usual prelude of whacking and pushing the wheels and reviling the animal's maternal ancestors, we at length made a start, my new gun resting carefully against the seat by my side. "Reveillé" was sounding in barracks, and a few natives wrapped corpse-like in their sheets were flitting down the misty Mall. A jackal, returning home from his nocturnal prowl, stole across the road. Once outside cantonments and bowling along the straight white road, a perpetual excitement was kept up by our meeting trains of bullock-carts laden with bales of cotton for the railway. As the drivers were mostly asleep on the summit of their loads, with their blankets well wrapped over their ears, it required a good deal of vehemence on mine and the syce's part before they could be induced to prod the lethargic bullocks out of my way into the deep dust on either side the road.

At the sixth milestone of the monotonous, tree-bordered road, whose only variety was an occasional collection of mud huts or a mango grove, I found the shikari squatting on his haunches in the dust, and looking somewhat cold. Here I left the cart, and shouldering my gun, started off towards the "jheel," across fields of low green bushes of "dal," across carefully tilled little patches of rising corn, and skirting tall crops of millet and sugarcane, over a sun-baked plain. Presently the ground fell slightly, and became cracked and caked like dried mud. My guide stopped short, and appeared bewildered. With some difficulty, I gathered from him that this was where he had expected to find the jheel, but that the water had mysteriously vanished, God only knew where, and with it the snipe.

Short as had been my residence in the country, my faith in the wild Hindoo had already received several fearful shocks. I, therefore, approached the shikari with alarming menaces of corporal punishment, and—despite his entreaties and asseverations that he knew no more of the whereabouts of the jheel than did I, "His Highness, the protector of the poor, his father and his mother," all rolled into one—informed the "son of a pig" that this was not Paniput Jheel, and that if he didn't take me there sharp it would be the worse for him.

This ebullition had the desired result. Resuming our march, we very shortly came on a tangled mixture of mud and morass, swamp and sedge, with here and there a thorn-bush or a clump of high grass stretching as far as the eye could see in a long serpentine line.

Forthwith from our rear the shikari evoked four coolies who had been stalking solemnly behind us wrapped in dirty sheets. These formed a line, with myself in the middle, and we started beating along the sedge and water on the edge of the swamp. The sun was now well above the horizon and had a good deal of power; the air was dead still.

Suddenly from out of a tussock of grass right in front of me, with a wild cry, like the creaking of an unoiled lock, rose a bird, ridiculously small to expect one to shoot. When I add that instead of giving one a chance by flying straight and fair it made three distinct twists, the reader will not be surprised to hear that it got away scot-free.

There was indeed no doubt about the snipe being in, and I only wished my eye had been the same. Now in wisps of four or five, rising together like a rocket and scattering like fireworks; now singly, sometimes at one's feet and sometimes out of shot, they went up in all directions. Still every one escaped me. The sun grew hotter. My feet and legs were soaked. My temper did not improve, but the snipe's chances did. The shikari accompanied my misses with *mal apropos* observations as to when to fire, which made me feel inclined to slay him.

But at last came a proud moment. One bird, with evidently better feeling than the others, rose well within shot, and, with a subdued twitter, made off slow and straight. The next minute he fell dead, and a coolie promptly retrieved him out the water. A poor thing—after such an expenditure of time and walking and cartridges—but mine own. I gazed lovingly at the long-billed trophy ere I hung him by the neck on the gamestick.

The discharge of a gun not far off startled me, and to my intense astonishment I beheld Shotwell and Cartridge emerge from behind a patch of elephant-grass. Their greetings were warm, but hardly cordial.

"You're a nice sort of chap! What do you mean by coming out on to our jheel?"

"I'm very sorry," I began, "I had no idea that in this country any of the shooting was private——"

"Bless the boy! I don't mean that. But the shikari ought to have known better. He knows we keep this jheel snug——" And Cartridge made for the shikari, who fled.

I interposed, for a light seemed to dawn upon me.

"Hold hard, Cartridge; now I think of it, he was not at all anxious for me to come here. He tried to put me off with a dried-up place across the hill."

Cartridge laughed. My innocence was so palpable.

"Well, and what have you got? You have been blazing away enough to scare every snipe out of the country."

Triumphantly I pointed to the game stick, but to my mortification evoked a roar of laughter from my brother officers.

"Why, man, that's not a snipe at all! That's a snippet, look at its white breast!"

And they both seemed so amused that I got proportionately annoyed—for after all one is not born a snipe-shot—and I was not sorry to find subsequently that my battue had so disturbed the jheel, that the two professors were unable to get near a bird, and were forced to give it up and beat a retreat homewards.

Cartridge and Shotwell lived in a bungalow next mine. As, later in the day, I was emerging soothed and amiable from a warm tub, a shot from their verandah startled the grey squirrels in mine. Looking out of the bathroom door I perceived the two again intensely amused over something. Their mirth was irritating.

At dinner time at mess the story of my first day's snipe shooting went gaily round, with embroideries various. Especially it seemed to tickle Fitzdangle (he is such a fool, anything will amuse him), who had made use of my absence to go over and lunch with the Dashingtons.

But Cartridge patted me on the back.

"Never mind, my boy, you'll do better next time! And I've told them to serve you for breakfast with one of the few snipe we really did kill, that you may see what it tastes like."

Next morning I came in late to breakfast, for I was stiff and tired with my walk and my wetting. The table was full of fellows, while others presently lounged in as if expecting something. My promised snipe, a plump little carcase mounted on fried toast, was brought in solemnly by the mess-sergeant himself. General interest was evinced as I ate it, and when it was finished everyone wished to know how I liked it. I remarked it was very well cooked, but rather dry and bitter. Fitzdangle sniggered again.

But at lunch Cartridge shouted across the table:

"Well, and so you liked the hoo-poo?"

"What hoo-poo?"

"The hoo-poo you ate for breakfast, thinking it was a snipe. Shotwell shot it in our garden, and we had it most carefully plucked and cooked!"

To this day the sight of one of those jaunty little birds, with his nodding perky crest, running about the garden, reminds me very unpleasantly of my exceedingly *mauvais quart d'heure* of chaff which followed Cartridge's disclosure.

However, to do him and Shotwell justice, I must relate that in order to encourage the young idea, they took me out the following week to Paniput Jheel again. We made a splendid bag (Cartridge shooting four birds with a right and left shot) of thirty couple, to which, however, I must confess, though the snipe rose steadier and flew straighter, I only contributed the modest quota of five.

Nevertheless, I went home in such good spirit that I couldn't resist, as I dressed for mess, shouting across to the doctor, with whom I share my bungalow, to ask him why my tailor Lappel was like a snipe.

Of course he gave it up, for the doctor is a Scotchman and a "carfu' mon" in money matters, but other people besides an impecunious subaltern will have no difficulty in perceiving that the similarity lies in their both having long bills.

MRS. DIMPLE'S VICTIM.

The hounds met at the Fox Inn, Nethercombe, and all the village was astir. Nethercombe was very proud of its gorse, which was warranted from time immemorial to hold a fox. One by one, then in twos and threes, red-coats and black, dog-carts and broughams, came down the village street and congregrated in front of the inn, where mine host was drawing his best March ale vigorously. Then there was a flutter, and the huntsman, and the whips, with the pack at their heels, were made way for by the crowd, and halted under the sign-board.

There was a brief law for the late-comers, filled in by greeting and chatting, and the Master led the way over the brow of the hill towards Nethercombe Gorse.

The last of the field was disappearing up the lane, leaving only a few second horsemen and hangers-on under the sign-board, when a smart dog-cart rattled up and its two occupants, hastily throwing away the ends, of their cigars, and divesting themselves of their box-coats, shouted for their horses.

The tall slim man with the fair moustache was Godfrey Okeburne, of the 150th Hussars; his companion was a brother officer, and they had driven over from the depôt at Alderminster.

The hounds were already rattling a fox about the gorse, by the time the two later comers had trotted up the muddy lane to the corner by the gate, and some of the field were industriously pounding up and down the rides, to the intense annoyance of the Master and his subordinates, as well as of Reynard.

At last, however, this latter succeeded in eluding them, and in sneaking off unperceived, till he was viewed away by a shepherd near whose hut he had incautiously ventured.

In another minute the hounds were put on the scent, and the whole field was squeezing through a gate and down a pasture, as if their lives depended on it.

Well to the front rode Okeburne, but the chesnut was fresh and hot, and had got her head up unpleasantly. She hurried at the first fence, taking it too much in her stride. At the next, a tall big bull-finch, with a deep ditch and a bank on the near side, she went with a rush. How she landed or rather did *not* land, no one ever could tell, for the next moment she was lying a struggling mass at the bottom of the ditch, with her back broken and her rider under her.

"Take 'un to the Vicarage, there's nowhere else for 'un to be took, and no doctor within five mile," quoth Chawbacon, who advanced with a timely hurdle, as Okeburne was dragged from under his horse, unconscious, and with one booted leg dangling helpless and broken.

So to Nethercombe Vicarage they took him. The Vicar was away for the day, and it was his daughter May who received the hurdle with its ghastly burden in the narrow hall. She made no doubt Okeburne was dead, and therefore there was real relief, that made the blue eyes dewy in her fair face, when Okeburne opened his eyes on it and the world a few moments after.

His first sight of life again—for it had been a nasty cropper—and as such it fixed itself in his memory for evermore. But it was some time before he saw the blue eyes dewy again though. Five weeks he lay a helpless prisoner at the Vicarage, mending his shattered limb, and all the while the blue eyes first gazed softly at him, then shyly, and then danced and sparkled as they met his.

After the five weeks were over and the mischief was done, though the leg was nearly mended, Lady Marcia appeared on the scene, full of dignified maternal solicitude for her younger and troublesome son, albeit she he had not thought it worth while to hurry back from abroad sooner to look after him.

She fixed May with a stony stare, before which the soft blue eyes fell.

"My nurse, mother," said Okeburne, uneasily.

"Indeed? I am *so* grateful for your kindness to my son, but if I had had *any* idea how much he was encroaching on it, I would have moved him at any price! *So* good of you!"

Young and unused as she was to the world, May felt the sneer and the blue eyes filled. Okeburne noticed it.

That evening, in the twilight, when Lady Marcia had departed, having made arrangements to send to remove her son on the morrow, May stood at the window of the little sitting-room and looked wistfully into the bare elm branches against the darkening sky. The rooks were cawing good-night, and the maid came in and fetched away the Vicar. Someone wanted him. May too rose to go.

But Okeburne, who had been drinking in the picture of her fair face and form against the light, sat up in his long chair.

"Why are you going?"

"Have you forgotten? It's choir practice night; I must go and look up the hymns in the study."

"Come here!"

She obeyed unwittingly. Had he not called her to do things for him for the last five weeks?

The next minute she found herself a prisoner; his arm was round her waist.

"Don't, Captain Okeburne—you'll hurt your leg—sit down—"

"Then sit here on the floor by me, darling! It's our last evening, and I've something to tell you—but I think you know it already—eh?"

* * * *

Three months later Captain and Mrs. Okeburne had left the depôt and embarked to join the regiment in India. Lady Marcia had forgiven them, and given them—her blessing. As for any increased allowance, it was not to be thought of. Godfrey had already run through more money than any of the boys, and if he chose to marry a girl without a penny, well, he must just go back and soldier in India again. Anyhow, it was something to get him married; it might steady him, though what he could see, &c., &c.

And that was just the verdict of the 150th when they saw Mrs. Okeburne. Certainly marriage did steady Okeburne, at first. Perhaps the fact that the dashing

150th happened to be at a very remote station, where there was absolutely nothing to be done except pig-sticking, helped towards his improvement. In any case, May was altogether happy.

But the month after which she was named came on apace in all its sultriness, and played havoc with her fresh English complexion, her sparkling eyes, and her spirits. Simultaneously Okeburne, whose curse in life had always been that he wanted so much amusing, found the even tenor of domestic life, which had been so sweet in its complete novelty, pall upon him. He felt positively relieved when the doctor ordered his wife up to the hills.

Okeburne escorted her thither, and one evening they arrived at Simree and put up at the hotel by the lake. May was much too fatigued to put in an appearance at dinner, and her husband went down alone.

The first person he saw in the long dining-room as he scanned the lines of people at dinner was little Mrs. Dimple.

Her bright black eyes greeted him mockingly.

"Come and sit by me, dear boy. It's ages since ——— And what is this I hear, married? Oh! how could you?"

Daisy Dimple was the daughter of one and the wife of another Indian civilian. She was not more than five-and-twenty, and everyone had heard of her and her doings in every hill-station in the Himalayas. She never went home, what need? India was better fun. The only use of England was to supply you with clothes. In the hot weather she took up her abode at some hill-station till it got too hot for her, and in the cold season she flitted from station to station wherever there were any balls or races or festivities going on.

Dimple had some appointment somewhere. His great characteristic was good-naturedness. Daisy had been engaged to half-a-dozen men before she married Dimple at seventeen. Her father, in a burst of parental indignation, rushed the marriage on in a week, or she probably would never have done it.

Wherever Mrs. Dimple moved she was followed by a faithful pack of "bow-wows," some of many years' standing. These she managed with such discretion that they never quarrelled, each having his times and seasons, and all of them called Dimple "Dick."

Before he went home Godfrey Okeburne had been one of the "pack" and a favoured member.

He had not been up at Simree again for ten days (which May spent chiefly in bed with fever brought on by the journey) before he was again enrolled in the faithful cohort by little Mrs. Dimple.

Bacchus taking the chair at a temperance meeting, a pterodactyl among the water-fowl in St. James's Park, or the inmate of a Turkish harem lecturing on the rights of women, could not have been more out of place than the poor child from Nethercombe Vicarage was at Simree. It is always the naughtiest of hill-stations, and that year, owing to the presence of Mrs. Dimple and others of her ilk, it surpassed itself. Happily innocence is as blind as love, and May Okeburne passed through the fire unscathed. Her health, too, somewhat shattered by the hot weather, and several bad bouts of fever, prevented her from going much into society, and she was only too pleased that her husband found some amusements. Poor child, she gave out innocently enough that she did not mind how much and how late he was at the Club playing billards. But Simree laughed in its sleeve at her, for it was very little that the Club saw of him; in fact for "Club," read Mrs. Dimple's little rose-coloured bungalow among the rhododendrons.

But Okeburne's two months' leave was nearly up, and he must return to his regiment. May was really unfit to face the hot weather again before the rains fell, and the doctor's wife, good soul, proposed to keep her three weeks longer with them. Okeburne agreed, in spite of May's begging to be allowed to accompany him, and ere his leave expired took himself off on a ten days' fishing expedition among the mountains. May, of course, was quite unfit for such roughing it.

One evening she and the doctor's wife came home from their airing carried aloft in their "dandies" along the Mall by the edge of the lake. It was crowded with people riding, walking, and being carried and the band was playing near the Assembly Rooms.

"I haven't seen Mrs. Dimple about lately," remarked May's companion.

"I hope she's not ill; but you're quite right, I haven't seen her since Godfrey left." And then she thought no more of the matter.

Two days later the doctor's wife proposed to make a little expedition out to a bungalow on a' small lake some few miles off, and send lunch there. She fancied it would be a change and do the girl good, for May had faded so terribly, as fair, transparent women do in India. Only brunettes, like Mrs. Dimple, aided by art, manage to defy the ravages of the climate.

May's bearers, with their light load, got ahead of the more portly Mrs. Smith and the others, and she found herself arrived first at a turn in the road whence she caught a lovely view of the lake embosomed in the hills, and the little bungalow on a terrace above. Figures were moving about—servants and ponies. Evidently someone was staying there.

Presently the unseen watcher, halting on the mountain's path, saw two people step from behind the "chick" which covers doors in India, and seat themselves on chairs in the verandah. In another instant she had recognised her husband and Mrs. Dimple.

Mrs. Smith's jampan bearers toiling up the hill were met by May in her jampan returning.

"It's so hot and open near the bungalow, I want to have lunch here under this tree, if you don't mind, Mrs. Smith?"

"Certainly, my dear. But how white you look! Here, quick, William, she's going to faint—some brandy."

"It's the heat, I think," murmured poor May. And that one white lie was all that her agony ever wrung from her.

Not quite all, though. For when unhealthy September came, and cholera swooped down on the 150th's station, it carried off May as its first victim. Mrs. Smith, bending over her at the very last, caught the words gasped by the blue lips :

"Oh! if he had only cared for me a little, I shouldn't have minded!"

LIZZIE : A SHIPWRECK.

SHE was my first love, Lizzie Baynes.

I remember her in a short, white-cotton frock at the tenants' ball we gave down at Bannicombe every Christmas, a most fascinating little maiden. Blankshire my elder brother (home, like me, from Eton, for the holidays), and young Terence, the village doctor's son had a great quarrel, almost amounting to a fight, over a dance with her. It was characteristic of Lizzie that she finally elected to dance with Blankshire, because he had a name all to himself,—meaning, of course, his title.

As we grew older my passion waned, for we saw very little of each other, I never being down much in Wessex except for the shooting ; and I rather fancy Lizzie disappeared to a boarding school in a neighbouring town. Then, one spring, going down from Oxford to bury myself at Bannicombe and read for my degree, I found her blossomed out into an exceedingly pretty, if somewhat vain and flighty, little siren. Her father, whose father before him had been land-steward at Bannicombe, was mighty proud of her.

Sometimes on a wet afternoon, or in the evening when I was sick of "mugging," I would wander over to the farm and have a smoke and chat with old Baynes. Somehow, I generally found young Terence there, and was amused to notice the paroxysms of ill-concealed jealousy into which the little minx would throw the poor young fellow by flirting a bit with me. So I saw how the land lay there.

A year later, running down to Bannicombe for a few days, while on a round of visits in that part of the world, the first person I met coming down the avenue as I drove up from the station was old Terence, the doctor. He had been up to the house to see a sick servant. He was in such a state of beaming delight that I could not help stopping to ask after Mrs. Terence and the tribe of boys. He then quite took my breath away by the announcement that Pat Terence, the eldest, and my former rival, had passed his examination for the army, and had that week been gazetted to some line regiment. Of course I congratulated the old man, marvelling all the time over the folly of the Cardwell competitive system, which brought penniless lads like this into the service, and wondering how on earth the uniform was to be paid for.

The next time I saw Bannicombe was after eighteen months' absence, shooting big game with Blankshire in the Rockies. The little village wore quite a festive appearance as I drove up from the station, the bells ringing and all the women and children at the cottage doors gazing and talking; for, as I discovered, no less an event had just taken place than the fair Lizzie's marriage to young Terence.

"An officer in the army! To think of that, my lord," quoth old Baynes to me with exultation. "Not but what my girl's pretty enough for a duke; that she is,— begging your pardon, my lord."

Good old fellow! She was the only loss among all the boys, and her parents and her brothers had worshipped her from her cradle.

Three or four years later I was idling away a few weeks at Simla, on my return from shooting in Cashmere, and while it was yet too hot to go after the tigers in the Terai. The evening after my arrival I found myself at a ball at the Viceroy's, and in a crush at a doorway, face to face with Lizzie Terence.

In spite of the elaborate ball dress, and the diamonds glittering round her snowy neck and shoulders, there was no mistaking the pleading violet eyes, the sweet childish face, which first turned deadly white, and then flushed crimson as she recognised me.

"Lizzie," I said, holding out a hand, "is this the way you treat old friends?"

She stopped and looked at me with an imploring look.

"Oh, Lord Archie! one does not expect to meet old friends out here," she faltered.

"If we are going to dance this, we had better begin before the crush comes."

The speaker was Major the Honourable Percy Standish, the smartest and most aristocratic of all the Commander-in-Chief's A.D.C.'s, black-browed and dissipated-looking.

All the years I had known Percy Standish about town, I had never liked him less. The familiar tone in which he spoke to Lizzie jarred upon me. They passed on, and some one behind me congratulated me on being an old friend of the beauty.

Remembering the imploring look of the violet eyes, I restrained a smile, and admitted to the honour of having known her as a girl, and knowing her people down in Wessex, suppressing all details, and marvelling over the elasticity of Anglo-Indian society.

"So she's the beauty?" I asked.

"Quite the prettiest woman this year in Simla," rejoined my informant. "Bad style, you know, but very fetching. Standish discovered her when the Chief was inspecting her regiment, and got her up here. But he's such a beastly selfish chap, won't let anyone else have an innings."

"The Viceroy himself was rather smitten," remarked some one else; "but Lady——(naming our hostess) put her foot down. She has so much to put up with, don't you know——"

And so on with notes and comments which won't bear repeating, and which made me feel sick at heart, as I watched Lizzie and her diamonds revolving with Standish.

I went to call upon her in her pretty little châlet, nestling on the hill-side among the rhododendrons. Poor Terence, she informed me, was grilling away in the plains somewhere below, and could not get leave. I met her everywhere, at heavy official dinners, at Benmore subscription dances, state balls, picnics, out on the fir-clad heights of Mashobra, and at sky races down in the grassy valleys of Annandale; at all the entertainments, in fact, which make up that mill-wheel round of dissipation called the Simla Season. For once the doors of the Viceregal lodge are open to anyone, all the other doors in Simla follow suit, and Standish had compassed the first requisite for Lizzie,—not that at any time it requires much management, for there is but one society in Simla, and that is elastic.

In public Lizzie was always very gracious to me, throwing over in my favour many of the lesser stars among her admirers; but when we were alone together she was embarrassed, ill at ease, and carefully kept the conversation off home and home subjects. I know not whether she was afraid lest I should divulge her antecedents, or take her to task, with the licence of an old friend, for her present behaviour. On the score of the former she need have had no fear, but the latter I felt sorely tempted to do, and watched anxiously for an opportunity, which she never gave me.

A week or two slipped away. One evening, about midnight, I started to walk back from the club to my hotel. I had been playing whist there part of the time with Standish, who, however, had complained of fever, and left early. It was a glorious Indian moonlight night; the cool night-breeze rustled in the deodars, and the sky was flooded with stars, while the nearly full moon cast inky shadows. It was all so lovely, I felt disinclined for bed, and lighting a cigar, strolled along the Mall under the rhododendrons. Suddenly, round an angle in the road, I saw before me a pony waiting at the foot of a zig-zag path leading up the hill-side, with a sleepy groom lying on the road beside him. In an instant I recognised the pony as one of Standish's, the one with the two white stockings I had often seen him riding. I looked up, and saw Mrs. Terence's house gleaming white among the trees. Before I had time for wonder, I heard a sound of voices, and a dark mass coming down the path instinctively made me slacken my pace. The dark mass evolved itself into a man and a woman. The former stirred up his groom with the butt-end of his whip, mounted the pony, and cantered off, the latter remained standing bareheaded in the moonlight looking after him.

Now was my opportunity. I quickened my pace, came up behind her, and laid my hand on her shoulder.

"Lizzie, what does this mean? What would your father say?" I asked, as sternly as I knew how.

She quailed and shrank before me, and looked around as if she would have fled. Then suddenly she burst into tears.

"You won't tell father, will you?" she sobbed. "It would kill him! I know I'm very wicked; but I must have excitement, and parties, and frocks, and Percy is very fond of me, and he's a lord's son, you know."

I hesitated for a moment what to do. Her tears unmanned me. I had never seen her cry.

"Lizzie," I said at last, "let me save you from yourself. Let me send you home to your father. I will pay your passage."

"O no, Lord Archie," she cried, with a shiver. "Not home,—I could not bear it. Bannicombe is so dull,— no dances, no men. No, anything but home." And she escaped from me, and fled up the hill.

The following afternoon, at the Senior Member of Council's weekly garden-party, I overheard a scrap of conversation between Mrs. Commissioner Crabtree and Mrs. General Backbite.

"There can be no doubt about it, I should say. We saw his pony waiting below the house a few nights ago as we were going to the Smiths' dance, and it was still there when we returned. Looks bad."

I turned and saw Mrs. Backbite wearing as vindictive an expression as ever I saw on mortal woman's face, and recollecting something I heard about her having great hopes last year of catching Standish for her daughter, I trembled for Lizzie.

That very evening I got a telegram saying my shooting party in the Terai was awaiting me, and had to rush off early the following morning without time to say good-bye to Lizzie. On emerging from the jungles some weeks later, and returning to civilisation and posts, I found my Simla letters full of a terrible *dénouement*.

A garbled story of an anonymous letter sending an infuriated husband rushing up from the plains, to find a white-stockinged pony waiting on the terrace by night: a locked door broken open; a fight between two angry men, and a wretched little wife turned neck and crop out of doors—all this came down piecemeal from my various correspondents, and made my heart bleed.

Before I left India the case came into court, and I read in the papers that Standish had been mulcted in a heavy sum (I suppose his relations helped him out, for I knew he had not got it), and only by bolting home without leave, and jeopardising his commission, escaped the two years' incarceration which the Indian law inflicts on similar offenders.

Of what had become of the erring Lizzie, not one syllable reached me.

As a change from the ordinary mail route, I embarked, for home in a vessel belonging to one of those foreign lines which coast up Italy. After the first few days when people on board had got over their sea-sickness and began to talk, I found much speculation rife as to a mysterious and lovely being who occupied a reserved cabin, whence she never emerged, and who had all her meals brought in to her, though she was not ill. I paid but little attention to the gossip, knowing how people make mountains out of molehills on board ship, for lack of anything better to talk about.

One night, however, when we were not far off Aden, finding my cabin unbearably hot, I came up again to sleep on deck about an hour after turning in. Emerging on the deck at the top of the companion, I found myself face to face with a figure wrapped in a shawl, pacing the deck like a caged tigress. There was no mistaking her, though she was worn and haggard, and her eyes shone like burning coals.

"Lizzie!" I exclaimed.

She gave a cry, and turned from me; but I held her fast.

"Leave me," she cried. "How can you speak to me? I saw you come on board, and I have been trying to avoid you."

"Why should you avoid me, Lizzie?" I asked, soothingly. "Come and sit down and talk to me. I am an old friend."

"Friend!" she repeated, with a harsh little laugh. "I haven't a friend in the whole world. Everyone shuns me; no one speaks to me. All because I've been found out. You can do what you like if only you're not found out. Percy's left me, raving at me because he's lost his appointment. They've taken my boy away from me; and you don't suppose Pat will take me back, do you?" she added bitterly, with an hysterical little laugh.

I tried to calm her, to induce her to go down below to bed, but in vain. Then, noticing she was shivering in her thin white gown, I offered to go and fetch her a warm rug. She looked up at me with something of the old pathetic look in her lovely eyes.

"You were always good to me! I wish I had gone home when you told me to."

It was quite a calm night, the tropical sea like glass; yet, just as I dived down the companion, I distinctly heard, though I hardly noticed it at the time, a splash of water, as if a wave had dashed against the side of the ship. Down below lights were out, and it was only after some delay I could find my rug in the dark. When I returned on deck, I was glad to find Lizzie had taken my advice, and gone, as the watch explained to me in his Italian *patois*. So I turned in too.

But with the next morning came a terrible hue and cry. The mysterious lady had disappeared. Her cabin was empty; her berth unslept in. There was but one solution of her disappearance, namely, the splash I had heard in the midnight Indian Ocean. I kept my own counsel, but it was perhaps with the feeling it was best that I had thus seen the last of the erring, lovely Lizzie, and that the waters had closed over her unhappy career.

> " Mad from life's history,
>   Glad to death's mystery
>   Swift to be hurl'd.
>   Anywhere, anywhere,
>   Out of the world.
>   In she plunged boldly."

* * * * *

A few days after I reached England the Turkestan war broke out, and among the list of killed in the first engagement I read the name of Pat Terence. The same paper contained the announcement that that gallant and distinguished officer, lately on the staff of H. E. the Commander-in-Chief in India, Major the Honourable Percy Standish, had been appointed military secretary to his cousin, Sir Benjamin Blazer, the new governor of Victoria.

I must leave off now, for Lizzie's boy, whom I have sent to school, and who always spends part of his holidays with me, is clamouring for me to go out and bowl for him.

HOW THE CONVALESCENT DETACHMENT KILLED A TIGER.

THE noble army of convalescents was *en route* for the hills. It is a thing of the past, now, that annual march of the blind, the halt, and the lame fleeing from the already furnace-like plains stations, for the railway now jogs along to the very foot of the Himalayas.

We were a motley crew. There were once-gay Lancers dejectedly trudging along on foot; gunners of every species; infantry of every coloured facing, including trewed Highlanders and Rifle Brigade, rusty with the dust. Day after day the weary little band trudged along the straight, dusty, seemingly never-ending road, towards the cool paradise whose faint blue outline fringed the long level horizon.

Bullock carts were goaded along laden with women and children, perched on the top of all their household goods, and covered over with a straw awning, leading a veritable gipsy caravan life. A long drawn-out line of doolies—those ferocious doolies of which *Punch* heard in the Afghan war as carrying off the wounded—each with its sick occupant tossing under its coffin-like roof, jolted along in the dust to the never-ceasing grunt of the bearers.

Foremost in the van rode the gallant major in command of the heterogeneous multitude in full glory of charger and trappings. About and behind him came the married captains and junior subalterns of all sorts, who had either volunteered or been ordered to do duty at the Convalescent Hill Depôt for the next six months, and to whom had been granted dispensations to ride on ponies, and who were clad in such variety of undress uniform as seemed good to every man in his own eyes. Mention must be made, too, of our "pill" and his apothecaries, whose time hardly hung heavy on their hands.

Trailing in front and behind the corps for miles along the dusty road came little groups of baggage animals. There were strings of camels tied to each other's tails, the foremost led by a native driver, a "drabby," with their vicious-looking heads and legs swinging about in all directions, and with rolls of tents balancing on each of their horny sides. Then came elephants with more tents, stalking along in an independent, business-like manner. Further on a string of mules, on their pack-saddles the men's kits in neat bundles, all ambling along on the look-out for mischief, for mules always seem possessed. Next came more bullock-carts with officers' baggage—the wheels creaking, the drivers shouting and whacking. Thus we moved along.

Already two nights had we encamped under the rows of mango trees which mark the Government camping grounds every ten miles or so, and had brought money and wild excitement into the cluster of mud huts yclept a village across the road. Two mornings had we been passed from time to time by the galloping "dâk gharry," a bathing-machine-like vehicle harnessed with two small ponies, and whose sleepy occupants, on their way to the hills, peered out at us. Who knows, perhaps one such conveyance contained *the* she who was to be the joy of our souls at ball, picnic, and ride for the next few months by the lake up above!

Before midday we are again settled in our canvas village as comfortably as if we had been there for a week. This camp was bounded on one side by a luxuriant thicket of bamboos. In a rude hut therein resided a filthy fakir—*i.e.*, religious person—whose earthly mission seemed to consist in daily feeding at sundown troops of jackals who assembled at his sounding on the cow-horn. This spectacle proved a mild excitement, for the men who turn out to witness it from the everlasting lotto game, or "house," the cries of which, "one, three, eight, fourteen, house," &c., had rung out unceasingly all the hot hours.

But in the major's tent—where at noon he had dispensed justice on a mule driver who had given one of his beasts a sore back with bad loading, and on a Tommy Atkins caught thrashing a villager who had dared to demand payment for some liquor—in the major's tent a solemn conclave was held. He a was real Highlander and had sporting instincts, but he was nothing to Jones of the 114th, who was young and bloodthirsty, and yearned to slay beasts not a whit less than Smith, a veritable old "shikarry," who looked upon soldiering in India as one long, shooting expedition, only that sometimes men were to be stalked and not tigers. These two urged on the major with the following results :—

THE CONVALESCENT DETACHMENT AND STRIPES. 173

In the Decalogue of the British army in India it is written that "on the seventh day thou shalt not march, but shalt halt, polish up thy kit, and do a bit of shut-eye." The major being very new to his responsible position, and somewhat of a Presbyterian, was inclined to a minute observance of anise and cummin. It took a little persuasion to get him to decree that halt we should, but that the Sabbath should fall on that day when we should be encamped at Sahari two marches off, in the heart of the Terai, a strip of marshy-forest stretching at the foot of the hills and the sportsman's paradise.

A further result of the conclave was the despatching of a native trooper, the major's orderly, with a polite request to the neighbouring Rajah of Panpore to have some elephants waiting for us at Sahari. We didn't know much about the Rajah except that he had elephants, and had lent them before, and that he resided in a metropolis some forty miles off surrounded with a cactus hedge, and where they made blue pottery. Civilians might have other views, but to the average military mind it is what Rajahs exist for. The conclave then dispersed, and there was a general tendency to look up rifles and cartridges. Young Robinson, just from home, sallied out secretly to try his brand new rifle, at the imminent risk of the villagers' cattle.

Sahari was a camp of evil odour. Its very appearance was malarious, and the sight of the forest officer's bungalow, perched up on stilts, as it were, to be out of the way of the miasma, was enough in itself to make one feel feverish. However, we all promised ourselves a dose of quinine at bed-time, and then the sight of the Rajah's elephants tied up in line dispelled every idea but that of sport. Presently we found we were in luck's way. There was a civil engineer in camp hard by, building a bridge over a refractory river. He was a devoted "shikarry," and allowed two elephants, which were used quite as much for sport as for their legitimate work. Then the forest officer himself was roosting for a day or two in his bungalow perch, and he was supposed as a matter of course to know the whereabouts of every tiger and herd of deer in his district, which was about the size of an English county. That is rather the *raison d'être* of forest officers; they are, as it were, gamekeepers on a large scale. To crown all, "khabar," that is to say news, of a tiger itself floated mysteriously through the camp. Some cow or other had fallen a victim only a night or two before, within a mile of the camp. Was ever such luck as ours? Everyone was on the tip-toe of excitement, and young Robinson had fearful nightmares of hand to hand combats with the lord of the forest.

It was cold, and raw, and misty, and barely light, when our bearer insisted on awaking us next morning; but as soon as we had collected our ideas sufficiently to remember the importance of the occasion, we turned out to a man. Outside the tents the huge beasts were drawn up in battle array, a patient mahout seated behind the ears of each. The private elephants carried neat, if narrow, howdahs, wherein two men, not overburdened with long legs, might sit with difficulty as in a narrow pew in church. But some of the Rajah's elephants had only a pad or mattress, whereon some of the youngsters were forced to maintain a precarious existence. Next came the mounting. It was all very well for the elephant to lie down, but that hardly seemed to make any appreciable difference in its height. Still the howdah towered above us, and ladders there were none. However, the animal was good enough to make a curl in his tail, using which as a foot rest we were able to haul ourselves up it on to his back.

Then the procession started. Fifteen elephants solemnly stalked through the brushwood, and through the jungle beyond the camp; crashing under boughs which almost swept one off the howdah, fording marshy streams, up the muddy fern-clothed banks of which the wary beasts would not venture till they had sounded them with their trunks and feet. After about a mile of this we emerged on a clearing in the forest, a patch of tall elephant grass some half-mile square. Two "stops" were sent round, one to each corner of the far end of the grass, and the rest of the elephants formed line to beat down the jungle. The two stops carried the major with the engineer, and the forest officer with Jones. We smaller fry mounted on the line elephants dived silently into the grass and the beat began.

All that we could see around were the other elephants' ears and their riders' sun helmets waving above the sea of grass. Screaming pea-fowl, whirring black partridge, quail, hog, and spotted deer fled startled from the covert under our very noses, and were allowed to escape. Suddenly, to the motionless watchers at the other end of the jungle, the grass appeared to wave as if from a mass creeping below it. A few minutes later and a patch of colour flashed on the outskirts of the jungle The next moment the tiger himself cautiously sneaked into the open. Then we in the rear heard the sharp reports of two shots. When we gained the open we found the triumphant major afoot measuring his kill : and as we crowded round him, we of his detachment felt a measure of his glory fall upon us. The tiger was laid across a pad elephant, and carried off into camp.

But the morning was still young, so short and sweet had the performance been ; so we remounted and beat again—for deer, this time. The jungle seemed alive. They bounded out on each side as we crashed along, and every minute the forest re-echoed with a shot. In fact, young Robinson on the front of veteran Brown's howdah declared himself deafened for life by the constant discharge of the latter's rifle in his very ear. Thus the morning wore away, till the sun striking almost vertically down through the branches—some of which, after the foolish habit of some Indian trees, are shedding their leaves in the spring—warned us to return to camp to tub and breakfast. We repeated the performance, minus the tiger episode, in the cool of the evening, and there was much feasting off venison in the men's tents for some days to come.

At dinner we made merry with the forest officer and the engineer, who lead such solitary lives, poor fellows, that they were quite uproarious. But we must turn in early, for *reveillé* will sound to-morrow with the first streak of dawn, and three-quarters of an hour later the bugle-call to strike tents. Nevertheless we pass out into the moonlight to gaze once more on the tawny skin of our prize stretched taut on the ground, previously to being rubbed with wood ashes to preserve it. The major has carefully removed the claws and whiskers, or the natives, who regard them as charms, would make away with them. One more loving measurement—for is he not our depôt tiger, the legend of whose demise will linger around the Convalescent Depôt for years to come?—and we turn in to a well-earned repose, lulled to rest by the bubbling of the camels seated in circles close by ready for the dawn, or the far off bay of a pariah and howl of a jackal, or a difference of opinion between two mules.

FAITHFUL UNTO DEATH.

THERE was a dead silence in the room, broken only by the ticking of the clock. The master of the house—the Rev. Theophilus Carr—stood with his back to the fireplace, his hands thrust into his trousers' pockets, and his eyes bent on the ground with a stern-set look on his face. Mrs. Carr, a pale, frightened little woman, sat at a mall table, nervously trying to do some fancy-work which trembled in her hands, and ever and anon stealing furtive glances at the others.

The central figure of the group was a good-looking young man, smart and well dressed in an irreproachable country costume of shooting-coat and knickerbockers. He had a thin face, perhaps rather worn for his years, a slight dark moustache, fine eyes, and dark hair already prematurely thin on the top. He sat nervously drawing diagrams on the carpet with his walking-stick, and his face wore a worried, harassed look.

Looking out of the window stood Mabel Carr, who looked the image of her father. She was a tall, slight girl, with her hands tightly clasped behind her back, and a hard-set look on her face just like his, only that her lips quivered now and then.

At last Mr. Carr broke silence.

"No, Godfrey, much as I like you personally as an acquaintance, I can only repeat what I told you when you called a week ago. I should not feel justified either as a clergyman or a parent in giving my Mabel to a young man of your antecedents. No, don't interrupt me. I dare say you are no worse than many, but I look for some one better than most for *her*." And here a softer look came over his face as he glanced at his daughter. "I must beg, therefore, that you consider all over between you, and that, for the present at least, all acquaintance between us cease."

Godfrey Allen barely heard him out. He sprang to his feet, and seized his hat.

"Well, then, Mr. Carr," he cried bitterly, "remember she would have saved me—me, the son of your oldest friend; but now I tell you I shall just go straight to the devil!"

And with one look of unutterable longing at Mabel he strode to the door and left the room.

Mrs. Carr gave a little shocked cry at his last words, and a nervous look at her husband.

Mabel didn't move till she heard the hall door slam; then she, too, turned and left the room without a word or a look. Her father's eyes followed her sadly to the door; then he flung himself down into a chair and took refuge in a newspaper, while Mrs. Carr began to cry quietly.

As Mabel closed the drawing-room door behind her, a slip of a school-girl sister, who had been waiting in the hall, ran up to her, and threw her arms round her neck.

"Dear Mabel, is it all over? Is he gone away for good? Oh! I know he has."

Mabel put her gently aside, and, fleeing upstairs to her room, locked the door behind her.

All the long golden summer afternoon the sunlight flickered in and out through the casement, and the bees hummed in the jasmine creepers. She could hear the mowing-machine at work on the lawn, and then the hammering-in of the tennis pegs. Anon came the shouts of her father and sister over their game. Her mother knocked hesitatingly at her door, but she gave no answer. The evening shadows lengthened, the cattle lowed in the meadows, the rooks came cawing home to the tall trees about the hall. Still Mabel lay on her bed, her wet face buried in the pillows, fighting out her first hopeless battle with cruel fate. At eighteen her life seemed darkened for ever.

Presently came Mary, the house-maid, (who also had a young man, and was very sympathetic,) with a cup of tea, which was declined. But she added in a hoarse whisper through the keyhole—

"A note from the 'all miss, please."

Even without the bright half-sovereign Mary had just then in her pocket, she, or any of the servants at the Hall or the Parsonage, would have done anything to help Godfrey and Mabel.

"Put it under the door," was the reply; and when her footsteps had died away down the passage, Mabel rose and picked up the note.

"I *must* see you to say good-bye to you. Meet me at seven o'clock at the boat-house.—Yours, faithful to death.—G. A."

The bitterness and anger faded out of Mabel's face as she read these words, and were replaced by a sad, heart-stricken look that was pitiable to see. She bathed her eyes and smoothed her hair and went down to the study. Her father was looking out the hymns for next Sunday. It was choir-practice night, and upstairs her mother and Nell were putting on their things to go to it.

"Father," she said, holding out the letter, "Godfrey wants to say good-bye. He won't come here: may I go down to meet him at the boat-house? I will come on to practice after."

He looked up at her face, so sad, so worn with the struggle, and, noticing the beaten look on it, with all the magnanimity of a conqueror he said:—

"Yes, child, you may go, but don't be late for practice."

Down by the river the shadows were growing dusk under the trees. The frogs croaked among the banks, and bats flew about. The skiff lay idle on the water, which was ruffled by the evening breeze. Over the meadows the mists were rising, and among the light bank of clouds to the east a pale light showed where the moon soon would rise.

Godfrey was pacing restlessly up and down the bank. When Mabel's white dress loomed under the trees, he went up to her and would have caught her in his arms. But she drew back, and putting both hands in his looked up in his face.

"Godfrey, I've come as you asked me—to say good-bye; don't make it too hard for me, I can't bear it."

"My darling!" he murmured. His voice shook, and he covered her hand with kisses. Then abruptly he put her away from him, and began walking up and down as restlessly as before.

"Good God!" he exclaimed, "it *is* hard that some people should have all they want and others nothing. Up there," and he pointed to the big house among the trees, "my brother has everything he can possibly desire; I am of the same stock, with the same bringing up and education. Why should he be rich and I a pauper? And why, just because I am a pauper, should I not be allowed to have the only thing I want, which would make up for everything else—you? And they talk of the justice of Heaven!" he added bitterly.

"Oh, hush!" said Mabel. "Perhaps it is best for you, who knows. Poor as I am, too, I should only be a burden to you, and you'll perhaps get on better without me."

"Mabel," he said earnestly, stopping straight in front of her, his hands thrust doggedly into his pockets; "you don't know what my life has been when you talk like that. It was not all my own fault; things have gone against me. But with *you* to live for, *you* to work for, I would and could have kept steady and straight! And you know it!" And his face lit up with a loving smile, and he drew her to him and printed one long kiss on her brow.

She drew herself away, but held his hand. Looking up into his face, she said quietly and solemnly:—

"Yes, Godfrey, I shall always remember how you loved me; and I shall never love anybody again as I love you. God bless you and keep you!" And she tore herself away and was soon lost to sight under the dark trees.

Godfrey stood where she had left him, watching her as long as he could see her, while a chill evening breeze stole down the river and rustled the branches.

Mabel walked swiftly over the park. The sun had set, the twilight lay brooding over the land. Nature seemed in harmony with her sorrow. Hurrying over the dewy grass, she startled the deer under the trees and the owls in the branches, and entered the churchyard.

There were lights in the chancel already, though it was still summer twilight out of doors. A sound of an harmonium and voices singing came over to her. She entered the church quietly by the northern porch. The nave was almost dark; no one noticed her. Echoing through the empty building came the voices of the choir :—

>The night is dark, and I am far from home,
>Lead Thou me on.

She knelt down in a seat, and, laying her head on the book-rest, sobbed aloud. Her life seemed darkened for ever. Yet she felt so young, and such a long, dreary journey seemed to stretch out before her, a journey to be trodden without him—

>O'er moor and fen, o'er crag and torrent; till
>The night is gone.
>And with the dawn those angel faces smile
>That I have loved long since and lost awhile.

But he seemed lost for ever. Never again would he smile on her. It was all over, this dream of theirs. No dawn would brighten for her. Never again was she to hear his voice and see his eyes fixed lovingly upon her. Fate had come between them. This hard, prosaic, worldly nineteenth-century Fate, which overlooked their wild, young love, and only thought of £ s. d., and asked: "What ye shall eat, and what ye shall drink, and wherewithal shall ye be clothed."

The music ceased, the children clattered out of the chancel, glad to be released. The old sexton began putting out the lights. Then steps came down the nave towards her. Mabel looked up. It was Christopher Trent, the curate. He stopped in surprise.

"You here, Miss Mabel? I thought you were not coming to-night."

Mabel rose and moved towards the door. She couldn't speak, and was glad it was too dark for him to see her face. But in the porch he seemed to notice something in her manner.

"The others are gone," he said; "let me see you home. You seem quite cold and tired." For she shivered in the evening air. "You won't mind my coming with you?" he added, with such pleading in his look and voice that she must have noticed it, had she not been too engrossed with herself, for the honest fellow suffered in seeing her suffer.

It was nearly a month after this that Mabel summoned up her courage and took the path to the boathouse again. She had settled down into the everyday routine of life. But there were dark circles under her eyes, and her cheek was pale, and she was listless and aimless. Sweet, gentle, and obedient she had always been at home, but her spirits were gone. Her parents marked all this, and said to each other: "She is young; let her alone. Time will heal all."

But her mother shed quiet tears over her sometimes. Nell never teased her now, and was more than usually devoted.

To-day, however, Mabel thought herself strong enough to allow herself the

> Pain that is almost a pleasure,
> And the pleasure that's almost a pain,

of revisiting the spot where she had said good-bye to Godfrey. But she chose the middle of the day.

Adams, the head gardener at the hall, who had known her since she was a baby, was pruning some creepers about the boat-house. She stopped to wish him good morning, though inwardly vexed not to have the place to herself.

"Weel, Miss Mabel," began the old Scotchman, "and begging your pardon, there are sair news fra Lunnon."

"What do you mean, Adams?" she asked quickly, for she guessed he meant news from some of the Hall people now in town.

"It's that sorra I am, Miss Mabel, as I dinna ken how for to tell ye. Maister Godfrey, indeed!—him as I mind when he was *so* high——"

"Master Godfrey, well, what of him?" and Mabel turned sharply and fixed her eyes on the old man.

"Yes, Miss Mabel, Master Godfrey. Why, ye must ha' heard sooner or later, tho' I grieve to tell ye. He's gone and 'listed for a soldier, the bonnie lad!"

The colour left Mabel's lips.

"Tell me quick, Adams, how did you hear this? It can't be true!"

"Ah! and I'd gie a guid deal if it weren't. But come straight fra' Lunnon, fra' my granddaughter Jessie, the lassie as is one of the housemaids at squire's, ye ken, miss, and it's ower true, it's ower true!" And the old man shook his head mournfully. "Ye see, miss, when Maister Godfrey went away from here so sudden, like a month back (and right sorra we were for the cause as made him gang awa', begging yer pardon, Miss Mabel), he went up to squire in town. And Jessie do say, as squire took on finely, and that they had words all along o' debts or money or summut o' the sort, and Maister Godfrey he left the house in a rage, and then next day he coom and tell the squire as how he'd gone and 'listed for a soldier, and squire swore he'd never spake to him again, and turned him out of the house. Ah! they twa lads, as I mind them, how they picked my flowers and stole my peaches. That they should ha' come to this!"

But Mabel had turned away, her hand clasped to her side, as if her heart would break.

Some weeks later, one grey morning in early autumn, with a tinge of winter rawness already in the air, Mabel and her sister were taking their daily constitutional along the dreary uninteresting turnpike road which ran between the fields and hedgerows of a flat agricultural landscape,

At the same time, in a busy southern seaport, a large white Indian troopship was getting up steam to leave the dockyard. The blue-peter flew at her masthead, and the broad gangway which connected her second deck with the jetty had already been withdrawn and replaced by a narrow plank. The poop was covered with officers in uniform, and a sprinkling of ladies and naval officers. The other parts of the ship swarmed with troops already, mostly in their rough, sea-going sailor-like kit.

They crowded the ropes, the deck-houses, and looked out of the port-holes.

Below on the jetty were groups of spectators and officials. The order had already been given for all for shore to leave the ship, and one after another tearful little parties had reluctantly come down the plank, and placed themselves on some point of vantage on the jetty, where they were still within shouting, or at all events within distinguishing, distance of their friends on board.

At last, however, even the small plank was removed the great hawsers which tied the ship to her moorings loosened, the last sailor jumped on board, and with a convulsive jerk of her screw the huge vessel began to move.

Then from all the hundred throats on board, first low and husky, and then swelling all over the vast dockyard, even to the town beyond, rose a true British cheer, which dimmed many men's eyes and made the women cry.

But Godfrey Allen, hardly recognisable in the rough blue serge suit and stocking cap of a private soldier, neither waved adieu to friends ashore nor joined in the cheer. There were doubtless many men on board who were leaving their mother-country under various circumstances of trouble, disappointment, and even crime, but none with half the bitterness that rankled in his heart.

* * * *

A year passed, and brought about great changes at Beeston Rectory. Mabel was leaving for ever. The stern, proud father has been suddenly struck down in a fit, and the crushed widow and her daughters had, after the sad lot of clergy-folk, to seek another house. It was now their last evening at the old Rectory.

Mabel, quiet and self-contained, but having within her an aching heart, had been her last round in the village. She had bidden good-bye to the poor people who had known her all her life, and amongst whom her father had toiled for so many years. She had knelt for the last time in the old church where she had been baptised, confirmed, and where she had once dreamt of being married. Then she had stood awhile at her father's grave, sad but quiet, with no other feeling than that of affection to the parent who lay there. Doubtless he had been hard and stern to her, but in many ways she was like him, and he had through it all been very fond and proud of his handsome daughter, and now all misunderstandings and hard thoughts were utterly forgotten.

Then came her last pilgrimage to the boat-house. It was getting dark as it had been on that never-to-be-forgotten night—one little year ago.

The Hall was shut up again: the great rows of windows, with the white blinds drawn down, seemed to stare coldly at her as she passed. She sat down on the rustic seat. The river flowed on sluggishly, just as it had done that night, and the breeze came up chill across the meadows. But Godfrey? Where was he? All these months, no news, no sign, no word of him. And so it was to be always, all through life! Her life was quiet and uneventful, and he had filled it up. She had not yet learnt to live without him.

She was not long alone. A figure in a wideawake and a long coat came to her over the grass. It was Christopher Trent, the curate, come to feel his way, with the love-light that she would not notice shining in his eyes.

"Miss Mabel," he began humbly, "I followed you here to get a quiet word with you, which I couldn't do in the house. You don't mind, I hope?"

She gave no answer. She would not help him. Perhaps she hardly even heard what he said; her thoughts were so far away.

"What I wanted to say," he went on, "is only this. I want to ask you to be kind enough to look upon me as a friend."

"Mr. Trent," she said, "you've been that to us more than ever during the last few weeks. I don't know what we should have done without you," she added wearily.

"Oh! but," he pleaded, "I want to be a friend to you specially. You are left quite alone in the world: you have a great charge in your mother and sister, and you have a great deal to bear. I ask nothing more than for you to look to me for any help I can give you—to treat me really as a friend."

A light seemed to dawn upon her. She looked at him sweetly, and pressed his hand.

"I will, indeed," she said frankly. "I never had a brother, but you shall be to me as a brother would have been."

Christopher sighed.

They walked home together silently. At the garden gate Nell met them.

"Oh! Mab, I'm so glad you've come in. I can do nothing with mother. She won't touch her tea, and you know she's hardly eaten anything to-day, and she'll be ill if she goes on like this."

* * * *

The Carrs settled themselves at a northern watering place, with rows of terraces and crescents, an esplanade, a pier, plenty of bathing-machines, and a regiment quartered up at the fort. Starcombe considered itself quite a first-class place. The Carrs were not poor, but not very well off. There was no necessity for the girls to do anything but amuse themselves, unless they liked, and Nell, who was growing up a very pretty girl, asked for nothing better. The girls in Starcombe divided their attentions between the curates at the ultra-high church down in the town and the officers up at the fort, and had rather a good time of it. But Mabel missed her quiet village life and her father, and Christopher Trent, and the poor, and the many interests in life she had at Beeston, and could not live only for flitting and dressing. Also, in a corner of her heart, she nursed Godfrey Allen still. Life seemed grey and dim, and she felt old and sad and dull beyond her years.

Yet another twelvemonth past, and Nell married a nice young fellow in the regiment at the fort. Christopher Trent married them. He ever hovered about the Carr family. Then Nell and her husband sailed away to India, and for a long six months of a dull dreary winter Mabel was the companion of her invalid mother, who was fast fading away—weakly and vaguely as she had done everything else through life.

Christopher Trent was a true friend at this time. His little visits formed the only cheerful break in Mabel's monotonous existence, and the sick woman delighted in him.

At last one morning, when she had sent Mabel out for a walk, Mrs. Carr spoke to him and drew from him the secret he thought he kept so well hidden.

"I can't last much longer," she said, "and I shall die happy if I can leave Mabel with you She has been a good daughter to me, and you deserve that she should be as good a wife to you. There was that nonsense about young Allen a long time ago, but her father was very firm and wise, and she has forgotten all about him now. There has never been any one else: she is not so attractive as Nell was."

"It has been the one wish of my life," sighed Christopher; "but it must rest entirely with her."

Presently Mabel came in, with a bright colour from her walk on the cliff in the east wind. Her mother took her hand, and drew her down beside her sofa.

"Mabel," she said, "here's Christopher Trent, weary with waiting, like Jacob. Won't you say yes to him and let me die in peace?"

Mabel raised her eyes—those deep true eyes which always spoke her thoughts.

"Christopher, I must have a few words alone with you first."

They went out again into the esplanade. People had mostly gone into lunch: there was no one about but the boat-men and the fly-men and the goat-chaise boys, and the goats and the fly-horses were eating their lunch too.

Christopher began. "I won't say much, Mabel; you know all I could say; I feel you do. But I've the offer of a living down in the East-end, a bad part of the town, with plenty of work, needing brave hearts and busy hands. Will you come and help me? I know it is what you would like. It is a noble sphere open for your energies, and, as for me, there is no other helpmate in the world I would choose."

They took a turn in silence, and then she stopped short and looked him full in the face.

"Christopher, you knew all about Godfrey Allen; but you may have forgotten—I can't forget: I never shall. For all I know, he may be dead, but his memory will never be dead to me. No one can ever be to me what he was."

Christopher bowed his head. "I know all," he said, "and I would not wish you to forget. I am content with you as you are."

"Dear, noble soul," she answered, putting her hand in his. "Then you must take me as I am."

Not long after the invalid faded away, one bright spring morning, when the east wind was blowing down the cliff, and the sea shimmering in the treacherous sunny glare.

A sultry June day in the soldiers' recreation-room of the 30th Hussars at Paltanpore. A burning wind blowing across barracks, with a breath like a furnace blast. Inside, thanks to the punkahs and the "kuskas tatties," screens in the doorways kept constantly wet, and through which the hot wind blew cool, the glass is only ninety-eight degrees. A few men in white drill uniform lounging about. One was seated at a table idly turning over an English paper, and reads as follows:—

* * * * *

"On the —th May, at St. Stephen's, Starcombe, by the Rev. David Carr, uncle of the bride, the Rev. Christopher Trent, vicar of St. Estaphe's in the East, to Mabel, elder daughter of the late Rev. Theophilus Carr, rector of Beeston, Berkshire."

The reader stares at the notice vacantly, then starts up like a madman, with a muttered oath.

That night he makes a beast of himself in the bazaar, and is taken up by the picket mad drunk and finds himself presently lodged in the cells for ninety-six hours.

* * * * *

The summer saw Mabel settled at St. Estaphe's in the East, in a little dreary house in a dull little square, an oasis of respectability among the surrounding desert of squalor and misery. All the gay world was out of town. The pavement was baking under the sun of a very hot August, and the world of brick and mortar seemed like a furnace to our country mouse. But Mabel was happy, happier, perhaps, than she had ever been since that fateful evening by the boat-house. She was very busy. The parishioners of St. Estaphe's never went out of town, and the harvest was very plentiful and the labourers very few. She worked among a population for whom there is no "season," and with whom care and want are ever at home.

But they gradually got to know her, and some of them to love her. A glimpse of the tall, graceful figure in its sober dress passing down some squalid court sent a thrill to many a care-laden heart that had almost forgotten how to feel pleased with anything but drink, while a look from those sweet eyes of hers brought comfort to many a sorrow-crushed heart that had ceased to expect any. And so on through the winter and through another summer. Not much time for thought or for looking back into the closed chapter of might-have-beens of the past.

One autumn evening Christopher Trent mounted his doorsteps, put his latchkey into his front door, opened it, and walked with a step that was very weary into the dining-room, where Mabel stood at the urn, and high tea was spread on the table.

He threw himself into a chair tired out. She brought him his slippers and a cup of tea. She stroked his thin hair, already plentifully streaked with grey, with a sweet smile that cheered him.

"My wife," he murmured, holding her hand, "what should I do without you?" Then he roused himself.

"That's a bad case of fever among the O'Learys down in Crumble Alley. I'm afraid it's typhus. They sent for me from the night-school. It's the eldest boy that's down, and the mother was like a mad creature. I promised I'd go back there this evening, for I managed to soothe them both a little."

"You must have something to eat first," was all her answer.

Within three weeks Christopher Trent had caught the fever from the Irish boy, and lay on his deathbed. His life, so nobly sacrificed, was ebbing fast. His last thoughts, his last words, were for his poor people; he grudged leaving them so, they needed him so sorely still. But his last look, as a smile of heavenly peacefulness which had its origin in things unseen, overspread his dying face, was for Mabel.

* * * * *

The 1st of January in India, Empress Day. On the brigade parade ground at Paltanpore all the troops are drawn up for the usual review. The General, Sir Harry Blague, of Mutiny renown, a handsome soldierly figure, with iron-grey moustache and close-cropped grey hair, rides down the line with his staff. First, he passed the horse artillery, a chestnut battery, very smart. Then came the 30th Hussars, the crackest cavalry corps in India. They have an Irish earl for their adjutant, and a sprinkling of scions of aristocracy among the officers, though the present colonel is only Wilking, son of the great furnishing firm. Indeed, they look a smart set of men in their dark tunics with yellow froggings, and the brass spikes of the white helmets glittering in the sun, while the horses champ at their bits. Then the general moves on down the line, inspecting the field artillery, an English infantry regiment in scarlet standing like a wall, and then a couple of native infantry corps in scarlet, with gay pugrees, looking most workmanlike.

Facing the line, gathered about the saluting post, where the royal standard floats aloft, is a mass of spectators in carriages, on horseback, and the natives in gay little canopied country carts. At intervals, keeping back the crowd, stand erect and motionless troopers of the 30th Hussars.

Behind one of these is a carriage, and from its occupants proceeds the following conversation :—

"Who's the tall woman on the chestnut Arab by the flagstaff?"

"Oh! don't you know, that is the good-looking widow just out from home—Mrs. Trent, I think, her name is!"

"Oh! yes, I know; she's the pretty Mrs. Fielding's sister in the 120th. That's the General's Arab she's riding. They say he's very much smitten with her!"

The trooper in front, standing like a statue, strained his ears to catch all this. His cheeks paled for a moment under their tan, and his eyes eagerly sought out the object of their remarks, and rest long upon her.

He was only Private Godfrey, nothing more, and never would be anything more. He was evidently a gentleman by education ; there were many such in the ranks of the 30th Hussars. When he first joined some years before, his captain, as usual, tried to give him a helping hand. But he was a disappointing man, strangely reserved and unsociable with his comrades, and with no wish to raise himself. From time to time he would break out into fits of wildness which would keep him back from the promotion he otherwise would naturally have obtained. There was no depending on him. Of course with his education he might have become a clerk had he chosen, and worked up in that line. But he seemed to have no incentive for getting on at all, though he was a good rider and a smart soldier if he chose. So finally they let him alone, and there he stuck, a private.

The General now returned to the centre of the long line, which stretched away on the dusty sandy plain. The troops presented arms and carried swords in a general salute, while the band, massed in the centre, played " God save the Queen."

Then the heavy guns boomed out so many rounds, and were followed by the feature of the day, the *feu de joie*. All along the infantry line flashes of smoke pointed skywards, followed by the sharp report, rush with the utmost precision up the front rank, and then back again down the rear rank.

The chestnut Arab which carries Mabel Trent does not understand all this at all. He is very fresh, and starts, plunges, and backs. At the second *feu de joie* he twists round and round in terror, but when the whole mass of troops take off their helmets, and wave them, giving three cheers for the Empress, it is too much for him. He lowers his head, kicks out, and bolts away from the dreaded sight, scattering the crowd before him. His first kick-up unseats Mabel, but her habit catches in the pommel and she is dragged along head downwards, a terrifying sight!

But as the Arab nears where Private Godfrey is keeping the ground, the latter dexterously gets in his way, and arrests his course. Then, watching his opportunity, gets alongside and seizes the bridle. Flinging himself from his own horse he frees Mabel, bruised and cut, and lays her on the ground. A crowd of friends and doctors, and help in general, close round her, while he remounts his horse and falls back into his place again.

To everyone's surprise Sir Harry Blague stops the parade till he has seen Mabel carried away home under proper care, and ascertained that she is not seriously hurt.

After the march past is over the regiments file away back to barracks. An aide-de-camp gallops up to Colonel Wilkins, who calls up the Adjutant. "The General wants to know who stopped Mrs. Trent's horse?"

Private Godfrey makes no sign, and they are unable to find out who it is, till, at the stable-hour which follows, a comrade divulges.

Colonel Wilkins sent the name up with these comments :—

"A queer character, very reserved and morose, supposed to be a gentleman, but no good, most untrustworthy."

The name of the trooper who had saved her life came, of course, to Mabel's ears. It struck her ear familiarly. Was it possible it could be he? She reflected for a moment. If it was he would make some sign. She sent word to offer him a reward for his presence of mind. But it was declined with thanks. He would not come to receive it. It could not, then be he. Also, Colonel Wilkins's account of Private Godfrey hardly suited the bright, high-spirited Godfrey Allen she had known and loved.

Weeks rolled on. Sir Harry Blague's attentions became more and more marked. Mabel dreaded every day that he would declare himself, and put an end to the pleasant friendship between them, for she sincerely liked the gallant old soldier.

Mabel's life at Paltanpore was not unhappy. She was a great help to her sister, worried with many babies, small means, and bad health, and no longer pretty and gay. The women and children of her brother-in-law's regiment found in her also a kind, sympathising friend, as they battled with the climate and exile and temptation. The small world of Paltanpore liked her too, for she was never given to uncharitableness and scandal-mongering, and her large heart sympathised with all.

. One day another big parade. This time a sham fight. Mabel viewed the mimic fray, riding about with the General and his staff, mounted this time on a thoroughly reliable pony. The feature of the day was a charge by the 30th Hussars, in which a soldier was thrown by his horse coming down in a hole, ridden over, and badly hurt.

That evening about dinner-time came the message Mabel had waited for all these years. It came at last.

Private Godfrey, the soldier who had been fatally hurt that morning, was dying, and had got permission for Mrs. Trent to come and see him.

She drove at once down to the hospital under a bright full-moon, which silvered the white dusty road and cast inky shadows. A moon you could see to read by.

A long, bare, white-washed room, the many doors open admitting the evening breeze, for the weather was already getting hot. Native hospital attendants in blue and red pugrees glided about with bare feet. An hospital sergeant in uniform led her to a small room on one side, where a dim lamp enabled her to see the figure lying on the narrow bed, and the face tossing on the pillow.

Would she have recognised it? Had she not guessed it was he? Hardly, perhaps. It was so worn and tanned, and the hair so thin and grizzled. Only the eyes as they opened now and then were the same.

"I don't think he'll last the night," said the apothecary to her as he came his round. The place was very quiet. A couple of orderlies from the dying man's own regiment waited about in attendance on him.

But he was no special chum or favourite with anyone, and they seemed merely to look upon their presence there as a matter of duty.

Mabel knelt down by the bedside, resting her hands on the coarse brown blanket. Did he know her? He seemed so restless; in such pain. But nothing could be done for him that had not been done. She took his hand, already growing clammy, and called him softly by name. This seemed to rouse him; his eyes assumed a sensible look, and rested long upon her. Then a smile spread over the weary face, and he tried to speak, and with a great effort he said, " Mabel! At last!"

After that he seemed quieter, but gradually sinking. All through the night she sat by his bed, wiping his brow, moistening his lips, and holding his hand. If she let go her hold he seemed to search for her.

One hour after another was struck on the gong at the guard-room in barracks, and the sentry's challenge of " Twelve o'clock, and all's well!" was caught up and repeated hourly in the still night. Pariah dogs bayed at the moon, and the jackal's chorus —

> Like crying babe or beaten hound,

or, as Byron has it—

> Like sound of midnight revelry,

echoed weirdly from some deserted spots. The moonlight flooding one verandah, travelled gradually round the building, and came in at the opposite one.

It was getting near morning. Already a faint grey streak showed in the east, and the inevitable crows were awake and beginning to caw in the trees.

Suddenly Godfrey roused himself again. A look came over him of his own self so many years ago. The fine eyes turned on Mabel with their old fire. Bending down to catch his words, his voice, though weak, seemed to her to have its old ring.

"I've spent a wasted life, Mabel, but I've been true to you. Faithful to death—good-bye—kiss me—Mab——"

It was the last flicker. Even as she pressed her lips on his there was a faint sigh, and the once strong hand relaxed its grasp of hers. Then some one came and led her away.

The next evening at sunset a funeral party entered the military cemetery of Paltanpore.

An Indian graveyard is not a lovely spot. Four high whitewashed walls keep out the jackals. Inside on one side are a crowd of monuments, on the other rows of nameless graves. Straight walls bisect the square, bordered with dusty, stunted shrubs, a few mango or cypress trees where the crows caw. Whether or not the place is well kept and cared for depends entirely on the chaplains, and they come and go. Here are no loving friends always living close at hand to wander in with sweet memorial flowers. For most of the dead have been laid here by strangers, and no eye that once loved them will ever look upon their graves.

Outside the gate stops the gun-carriage, with its six artillery horses and riders. The band ceases the "Dead March in Saul," to which the long procession had slowly paced from the hospital. The couple of officers belonging to the dead man's troop, who vote the whole thing a bore and want to be off to polo, stand chatting, while the plain coffin covered with the Union Jack, with the sword and helmet of the deceased upon it, is lifted down and borne upon the shoulders of six comrades. Outside the gate, too, waits "the masterless steed," which has been led behind the coffin with the jack-boots reversed in the stirrups. The chaplain comes to meet the *cortège*. It is a sickly year in Paltanpore, and he has many funerals. He hurries over the service as he leads the way to one of the two graves always kept ready and open in every Indian cemetery. Behind the coffin follow the troop in full dress, and on one side the grave the firing party range themselves.

A tall woman's figure in black is hidden behind a tree not far off. She hears the chaplain's voice gabbling the service, through the short Indian twilight which is already falling. Then the sharp report of a volley of carbines startles the rooks who are going to bed. Then the band strikes up a few bars of the "Resurrection," then another volley rends the air, a few more bars, and a final volley. And then the whole of the grand old air rings out its message of hope and peace. Mabel's eyes look up to the dark blue vault overhead, where the stars are beginning to twinkle, and feels that indeed yet another *reveille* trumpet call will sound again for her soldier and herself. She stands there yet awhile, musing mournfully, but tearlessly. Women, like her, who have suffered much, have exhausted their tears.

Presently outside the cemetery she hears the band striking up again, but this time some merry popular air, which jars upon her. The released officers gallop off, and Private Godfrey is as good as forgotten.

Mabel lays a large white cross of roses on the grave which two half-naked natives have just finished filling in, and then turns to walk home up the now moonlit Mall.

Presently she hears a horse canter up behind her and stop. The General jumps down and gives it to the native groom.

"Good evening, Mrs. Trent. I met your carriage going home just now, and they told me that I should find you walking here. I am so glad to have the opportunity of speaking to you alone. It is what I have been looking for for so long."

She gave a gasp as if in pain. The man did, indeed, pain her by speaking to her *now*, and it pained her, too, to have to give him pain.

"I am a battered-about old fellow," he continued, "and you are yet young and lovely. I feel it is presumptuous for me to dare to speak to you at all. But I want to offer you my heart with all the devotion a younger man could possibly feel, and to entreat you to make the remainder of my life happy. I have never cared for any woman before, or thought of any as I think of you," he added softly.

"But you care for me, I feel you do. Then listen to my story," she replied, turning round upon him. And, standing there in the moonlight with her sweet eyes fixed earnestly upon him, she told him all. As she proceeded, the fine old grey head, which had always been held so high before all the world, bent lower and lower in despair, and the steady hands nervously drew patterns with the cane in the dust.

When she had ended, the old soldier raised her hand reverently to his lips, and left her in silence.

* * * *

Far away from the lonely, nameless grave at Paltanpore one of the most devoted of the zealous sisterhood of St. Estaphe's, in the East, is Sister Mabel, toiling on—

> O'er moor, o'er fen, o'er crag, o'er torrent, till
> The night is gone;
> And with the dawn those angel faces smile
> That I have loved long since and lost awhile.

THE HAUNTED BUNGALOW.

A Story founded on Fact.

Colonel Rylstone was one of the best-known and most popular men in Blankshire. Every winter he came down to a little hunting-box in the centre of the best part of the country, and no one rode harder or was more genial and cheery in the hunting-field. Every autumn he had a moor in Scotland, and three or four Blankshire men were sure to be among the succession of guns he entertained there. Yet Rylstone, with all his popularity, was the despair of the mammas of Blankshire who possessed marriageable daughters. Still in the prime of life, good-looking, well off, and good-tempered, he seemed only to need a wife to make him quite perfect. But he appeared absolutely impervious to the charms of the Blankshire maidens. He would fill his little house with nice men for the hunt ball in the winter, and be profuse with theatre dinners and Hurlingham and Sandown tickets to his Blankshire friends who came up in the season. But thus far he would go, and no further; and Blankshire matrons heaved sighs of despair when they spoke of him. Why on earth didn't he marry?

One August, when all the gay world is at Cowes or Homburg, I happened to find myself down at Dressington-by-the-Sea from Saturday till Monday. Everyone knows what Dressington is like the first week in August; elaborately got-up Jewesses with foolish Gentile youths in tow; overdressed Gentile maidens, who have temporarily ensnared Jewish youth—short, swarthy, and irreproachably got-up, oozing money from every pore. Among such a horde on the parade, after church, I was amazed to run against Colonel Rylstone, of all men under the sun; and Colonel Rylstone walking by the side of a bath-chair!

Now, the bath-chair contained neither an aged relative likely to pop off suddenly with the gout nor a pretty and interesting invalid. In it sat a man whose age would be difficult to define. His face looked young, though his hair and moustache were perfectly white. His eye was vacant and lack-lustre, his expression utterly vague and meaningless, and his face was contorted every few moments by a terrible twitch. A more distressing object could hardly be seen.

Colonel Rylstone's greeting was cheery and cordial, but he followed it up by no invitation to come and look him up at his hotel or to dine with him. It was by a mere accident I found he was staying at The Grand, where I was, and even then I could see nothing of him. He was in constant attendance on the shattered wreck of humanity in the bath-chair. He ate with him, sat with him, walked with him, and it was only, I presume, after he had seen him put to bed by his male attendant that the Colonel turned up late in the smoking-room. He drew a chair up to mine, and lit a cigar, with a worn—distressed look on his face, very foreign to his usual expression.

"You look tired, Rylstone," said I. "Down here on duty, I suppose?"

"Yes, indeed, on duty—a most painful, distressing duty, one which darkens my whole life, or rather the original cause of it does. Did you see that poor fellow in the chair?"

"I did, indeed."

"Well, some twenty years ago he was the crack subaltern of my old corps, the Crimson Cuirassiers, and a better fellow, a smarter soldier, and a finer rider you couldn't find in all the three Presidencies. We were quartered in India then, at Punkahpore."

"His head seems affected now. How did it happen? Drink?"

"Never met a soberer fellow than Alan Ardshiel. No, it was a joke, a blackguardly practical joke. I'll tell you about it if you like. If you thoughtless young fellows with your chaff and your practical jokes were to take a lesson from it, it might do some good."

Rylstone in a moralising mood was something so new to me that it was with some curiosity I prepared to hear his story, while he poured himself out a preliminary whisky-and-soda.

"Punkahpore was not a lively station as regards society," began the Colonel. "There were plenty of black-buck to shoot and pig to stick, but not many ladies to flirt with. The 'Crimsons' were not a very much married corps. The Colonel's wife was in England, and the Major's too much occupied with her babies to be interesting socially. The Commissioner's wife was fat and pompous, and the Police-officer's decidedly 'touched with the tar-brush,' as we say in the East. So there was much rejoicing amongst us youngsters when Alice Thornlegh, the doctor's daughter, came out to him from her school at home. She was just eighteen, and such a pretty girl with a fresh peach-like complexion and gold-brown hair, a 'sight for sair een' to us, sick of the pasty-faced beauties of the East; and she was so deliciously fresh to everything, so overflowing with spirits and fun, that she seemed to breathe fresh life into the social languor and stagnation of Punkahpore.

"Of course all we subalterns fell in love with her at once. For the space of about a month she retained a paramount place in all our affections, and we all hated and all were jealous each of the other. But, after that time, as is the manner of healthy British boys, soldiering, sport, and cricket resumed their natural sway over us. But not over all. On three of us Miss Thornlegh had made a more durable impression. Charley Chiverton was one: the senior subaltern, a dark-browed, rather morose fellow, given to bullying at school, fellows who had been with him at Eton said, and certainly not popular in the regiment. Nobody ever went, in any scrape or difficulty, to Chiverton for help. No one ever appealed to him to do a turn of duty or a guard for him; for Chiverton would certainly have found some excuse for declining assistance. But he was a good-looking fellow enough, and for a while Miss Thornlegh seemed to admire his dark, inscrutable eyes, and rode and walked with him a good deal, and chose him on her side for croquet.

"Alan Ardshiel was quite as much devoted to the pretty Alice as Chiverton, but, unlike Chiverton, he did not attempt to conceal it. His was a sunny, frank nature, and he was too palpably happy in her society, too evidently wretched away from her presence, for his 'penchant' not to be known all over barracks.

"Ardshiel was my great chum ; we always did everything together, and shared a bungalow. If it had been anyone but he, I might, perhaps, have taken a more prominent position in the race for Miss Thornlegh's favour. But how could I find it in my heart to compete against old Alan ? And then, one evening, I found out quite by accident that it would have been perfectly useless, for he was first favourite.

"We had been to a moonlight pic-nic, to the ruins of the Dilkusha, a ruined palace a few miles away from Punkahpore. We had the table placed on the stone terrace, the flags of which were crumbling and splitting, and were the noontide haunt of lizards. The regimental band played from a shaky stand in the quaint, formal garden, a mass of weeds and creepers. The glorious tropical moonlight flooded the whole scene, making everything as clear as day, and the old palace stood out as if built of marble instead of stucco.

"After dinner, as we sat smoking on the terrace, I discovered Miss Thornlegh was missing, and the question was with *whom*, for Chiverton and Ardshiel had likewise vanished. I considered it my duty to ascertain with which she was walking round the weed-grown paths. If it was with my chum, nothing should induce me to spoil sport. But if it was with Chiverton —well, then—

"The shadows that the brilliant moonlight cast under the orange and mango trees, and over the stagnant green water in the stone-edged tanks, were black as ink. I lit a cigarette, and wandered on my search. The crickets whirred in the branches overhead, the disturbed frogs splashed in the water, as I passed by; the distant bay of a pariah dog, or howl of a jackal, echoed over the plain. Then there came a low murmur of voices. Two people were whispering, their heads very close together, and across the tank, on a stone bench, I dimly discerned two figures in the shadow. The next moment I recognised their voices. It was Ardshiel and Alice. Never mind what they were saying, my boy. Very much what you and I would say under the same circumstances to the girl we loved, I fancy. It was enough for me, and I turned away, very sick at heart. As I did so, Chiverton stepped out of the shadow not many yards ahead of me. I saw his face as he crossed a patch of moonlight, and a more evil expression I never beheld. He must have overheard Alice and Ardshiel's conversation as plainly as I had.

"I went back to my bungalow. I had no heart for the pic-nic now, the chatter of the party would be intolerable. Chiverton's bungalow was next to ours, and he must have come back soon after I did, and have had an altercation about something with one of his servants, for I heard sounds of angry voices, much bad Hindoostanee, and worse language, accompanied by the yells of the wretched domestic who was being chastised. The man went to hospital next morning, sick.

"Ardshiel returned very late, and in exuberant spirits. He came into my room and wanted to talk. But I pretended to be asleep.

"The following afternoon Mrs. Thornlegh and the doctor had a croquet party on the carefully tended bit of lawn in front of their bungalow, which had to be irrigated every night by little runnels from the well, to be kept green at all. I did not play, but took a melancholy pleasure in watching the way in which Chiverton with the whity-brown wife of the police-officer on his side, mercilessly croqueted Ardshiel, who was playing with Miss Thornlegh. After the game we all sat in the verandah and discussed cigars and pegs, in the short Indian twilight. Somehow or other, by one of those unaccountable freaks of fate which so often seriously affect our lives, the conversation fell on ghosts and ghost stories.

"'India's not a bit ghostly or weird,' remarked Miss Alice. 'I don't believe there's such a thing as a real, proper, blood-curdling ghost in all the country.'

"'Neither do I,' echoed Ardshiel, who would have agreed with her if she had sworn black was white. 'I never heard of an Indian ghost.'

"'O, but I have,' put in the Commissioner's wife, a fat lady who considered herself of great local importance, and had a many years' experience of the country. 'Why in this very station there's one.'

"'Indeed?'
"'Where?'
"'What?'
"'Do tell!' cried everybody at once.

"Mrs. Postlethwaite was only too delighted to air her knowledge. She nodded sagely.

"'Well, and indeed, I've always been told that that big old bungalow, next to the Native Infantry lines, is haunted.'

"'What by? What kind of ghost? Black or white?'

"'O Mrs. Postlethwaite, how awfully interesting!' added Alice Thornlegh.

"'Haunted by many ghosts,' pursued the great lady, 'I've always heard say, ever since my husband the Commissioner first came to this district. There was a massacre of European women and children there in the Mutiny time. The rebels caught them and shut them up there, and then slaughtered them. That is certain, anyhow. And the bungalow has never been lived in since, and no natives will go near it after dark. They say it's haunted.'

"'O dear, I feel quite frightened!' cried Miss Thornlegh.

"It was very dusk in the dim verandah, but I could have sworn that Ardshiel caught her hand and held it in his to reassure her.

"'What nonsense!' he said. 'I don't believe it. These niggers are such liars and such cowards.'

"'Not more superstitious than some of you Highlanders are,' sneered Chiverton. 'With all your bragging, I don't believe you'd spend the night there yourself, Ardshiel.'

"The Scotchman's blood was up.

"'If we Highlanders are superstitious, we are, anyhow, just as plucky as you cockneys, and more so, as I'll soon show you. What do you lay me I don't sleep in that bungalow to-night, Chiverton?'

"Chiverton laughed a low, unpleasant laugh.

"'My dear fellow, I really don't want to rob you.'

"'Then I'll do it without any money on, as you're so deuced certain about it. Bragging, indeed! Do you suppose I care a rap for a pack of natives' lies?'

"Chiverton got up and lit a cigar slowly.

"'Nothing easier than to prove you don't, my dear fellow. In the meantime, I must say good evening, Mrs. Thornlegh. I hear the "dress" for mess sounding,' and he walked off slowly.

"'Confound that fellow, with his irritating sneers and cool ways!' said Ardshiel. 'But he'll crow in a different key to-morrow morning, for I shall send my bed over to the old bungalow to-night, and sleep there.'

"Alice looked imploringly into his face.

"'You wouldn't have that fellow Chiverton think me a coward, would you?' he added.

"'No; certainly not,' I put in. 'I'll go and sleep there, too. He might be up to some larks, if you were alone—who knows?'

"'But, Mr. Ardshiel,' Alice added piteously, 'supposing it's true—supposing there is something—those poor creatures massacred—it's horrible!'

"'It *was* horrible, you mean, Miss Thornlegh,' Ardshiel corrected in a softer tone. 'But don't be alarmed. I beg of you. That frightens me much more than any idea of ghosts. It's not very likely that we shall be disturbed by anything but flying foxes and owls, or perhaps a jackal or two; and I think Rylstone and I are a match for any other flesh-and-blood visitors. I'll come over to *chota hazari* to-morrow morning, after your ride, and tell you all about it.'

"Thus we said good night and departed, with many a gibe and jest flung back as we walked down the drive. I can see Alice Thornlegh now, standing framed in the creeper-covered arch of the verandah, and waving her hand to us.

"Of course our adventure was an excuse for champagne at mess, and after dinner we were escorted to our new quarters by quite a *posse* of Cuirassiers, with lanterns. Our bearers had carried our beds there in the daylight, but nothing would induce a single native to accompany us there that night.

"The haunted bungalow was at some distance from the other European residences. It was all that was left of the station after the rising. The other houses had been fired and burnt to the ground. Only this one remained intact, for the ghastly reason that it had served as the prison and the slaughter-house of the helpless European females.

"It stood back some way from the road; the drive was grass-grown and overhung with untended trees. The roof was falling in in places, the verandah overgrown with creepers. It certainly did not look inviting.

"'We are much more likely to be bitten by a "*krait* than to be visited by ghosts!' cried Ardshiel.

Shoo! shoo!' and with a cheery yell he chased out a great white owl, which fled hooting.

"Our little camp-beds had been placed in the middle of the huge centre room of the bungalow, a gaunt apartment with the lofty ceiling supported on four large pillars, which threw queer shadows about the room.

"One by one our escort departed, and we found ourselves alone, the feeble flicker of a native oil-lamp alone lighting up the apartment. Ardshiel threw himself on to his bed.

"'By Jove!' he cried, 'I swore I'd *sleep* in this haunted bungalow, and I *shall* do it too, for I never felt more sleepy in my life; the champagne went pretty freely round at mess, and I was up at four this morning walking till breakfast after the snipe out at Paniput Jheel. So good night, old chap.'

"He pulled off his mess jacket, and in five minutes I heard him snoring. Ardshiel always was such a fellow to sleep.

"But I was more wakeful. A bat would keep skimming past my face; an owl hooted at regular intervals in a mango tree outside. I had an uneasy feeling that the place was full of noxious insects and reptiles, if of nothing worse. The jackal chorus in a corner of the deserted compound sounded weird and eerie. But at last I dozed, and then, it seemed to me, I had a dream. I dreamt Chiverton stole into the room—Chiverton, who had not come with the rest to see us installed in our ghostly quarters. I dreamt I saw him bending for a long time over the bed on which Ardshiel lay sleeping peacefully—the sleep of the light-hearted and happy. It was a fearfully vivid dream—could it have been reality?

"After that I must have slept soundly, for when I woke again I awoke sharp and alert, startled into sudden and complete consciousness by the most appalling sound mind can conceive. It was a wild shriek as of some creature in mortal peril—it was the heart-rending cry of a child in agony.

"I sprang out of bed in a second, and as I did so my foot touched something on the floor—something cold and clammy—not a toad or a snake—but, O horror! clearly visible by the flickering lamp, a child's foot, cut off and gory, but still encased in its little shoe; and all around the floor was covered with splashes of blood.

"I stood a few seconds struck still with horror. Then, again, the horrible cry of torture sounded, close behind me this time, and, impelled by an irresistible terror—the like of which I had never felt before, and pray Heaven I may never feel again—I fled into the verandah, out into the night, down the drive. On the high-road I stumbled and fell; my overtaxed nerves gave way, and I fainted.

"The dawn was breaking in the east when a coolie going to work found me, and gave the alarm to the guard. I only felt thoroughly myself again when I found myself on a bed in the guard-room, with wet cloths on my head.

"Then only did the cowardice of my flight break upon me in all its enormity.

"'Ardshiel!' I cried. 'For God's sake go and look for Mr. Ardshiel! He's still in that awful room!'

"They went to look for him, and they found—" (here Colonel Rylstone's voice broke, and he was a moment or two before he could proceed,) "they found 'the thing' you saw in the bath-chair to-day, with blanched hair and vacant grin and chatter, and palsied features. What he saw, what passed in that room, no one will ever know this side of eternity, for that shattered wreck was all that was left of my cheery, sunny, happy chum."

"But why on earth didn't he make a bolt for it, as you did?" I asked.

"Why?" repeated Rylstone, and he sat bolt upright in his chair and glared at me. "Why? Because *when they found him he was bound hand and foot, and tied down into his bed!*"

There was a silence, and Rylstone took another peg, a pretty strong one.

"And what became of Chiverton?" I asked, after a pause.

"That is not his real name. If I were to tell it you you would recognise a man well-known in the service, an able soldier, who has climbed to the top rungs of the ladder. Such is life!"

I hesitated a moment, and then I asked—"And Alice?"

Rylstone's voice changed from a bitter tone to a soft one.

"That autumn the cholera swooped down on Punkahpore. We 'Crimsons' were sent out hurriedly into cholera camp in small detachments. When I got back to the station after some weeks, Alice was lying between the four mud whitewashed walls of an Indian cemetery."

CHRISTMAS WITH THE CRIMSON CUIRASSIERS.

It was the last night of the voyage. With to-morrow's dawn the look-out on the maintop would spy the mighty Ghauts, the ramparts of India, fringing the eastern sky. It was a perfectly still, warm, tropical night, dark as Erebus, save for the light of the star-strewn heavens. Two young people leant over the side of the vessel watching the white phosphorescent pathway which stretched behind her stern.

"I'm awfully sorry the voyage is over," quoth he. "I wish it would last for ever."

The girl's face clouded.

"I am too; it has been great fun, and I don't quite know what is coming next. *You* are going back to your regiment, your friends, your horses——"

"And you to your father?"

"Who is only a name to me. I have not seen him since my mother died, when I was only three. And then I'm told he's very difficult to get on with, though perhaps I ought not to say so. But they call him the Iron Colonel, you know, and then a father is not like a mother; and I've no mother, I've nobody."

Her voice was so sad, though it was too dark for him to see her face well, close as he was to her, that Jack Harrage would hardly have been human if he had not been tempted, more strongly than he had been all the voyage, to say something very foolish and very irrevocable.

But fortunately at this juncture the tea-bell rang, and a clatter of tea-cups, enough to drown any sentiment, came up through the skylight. In addition, Cramwell, the young competition-wallah, who didn't like Jack and did like Nina, came up and asked the latter if she was not going to have any tea. So all Harrage could whisper, as they all moved down the deck, was—

"Don't say you've no friends. You know you have devoted ones. Perhaps some of them will come and look you up at Dustypore, if they may."

All the answer he got was a look, but that seemed to satisfy him.

Surely some one or other was very much to blame for having, in the twenty-eight days during which they had been cooped up together on the P. & O., allowed this girl of eighteen, fresh from school, and this penniless subaltern in an infantry regiment, to fall thus irretrievably in love with each other. But, anyhow, the mischief was done.

The Crimson Cuirassiers were not much married, or much addicted to ladies' society. But they happened this Christmas to find themselves stationed at that extremely solitary little place, Dustypore, which, in the native mind, is associated with the birth of Krishna; in the European, with the death of wild boars. There was no other regiment, and only three ladies in the place. One was the Police-officer's wife, "touched with the tar brush," as the saying is, and who had never been out of India; the second was the Quartermaster's wife, whose mind centred in her kitchen; and the third was the Collector's wife, with no mind at all, only a giggle.

Such being the state of affairs, it is to this day involved in mystery as to who started the idea of a ladies' dinner at mess on Christmas Day. I am inclined to think it was Dolly, the youngest sub., freshest from home, and with a hidden love for feminine society still lurking under his stable jacket, and not yet entirely suppressed by that of polo-ponies, Rigbys, and squadron movements. I rather fancy, too, he was actuated solely by a wish to spend a pleasant evening with Miss Nina, the Colonel's daughter, just out from home.

Be it how it may, the scheme received very general approval. Fellows felt they ought to give some sort of entertainment to the station, and those who were averse to it took three days' leave and went out shooting.

Stern and hard as his nickname implied, the Iron Colonel would have been less than human if he could have resisted his little daughter's sparkle of delight as he casually remarked, over a cigar —

"The fellows are talking of a ladies' dinner at mess on Christmas Day. I suppose you don't want to go?"

He himself had hardly dined at mess if he could help it since he commanded the regiment.

* * * * *

Christmas Day felt very strange to Nina when she awoke to find the sunlight streaming in through the deep verandah and open door; the black ayah crouching by her bed; the room huge, bare, and whitewashed. The only sign of rejoicing was in the decorations put up by the servants, and which took the form of garlands of marigolds strung by their stalks across the portico and the gateway. Outside, the crows cawed incessantly, and the trumpets rang across from the barracks.

Nina's mind wandered back to former English Christmases, and she came to the conclusion India was unsatisfactory, and not half as nice as the voyage out had been.

"Will you come to church with me, father?" she asked timidly, as he entered the drawing-room, the bearer fastening his gold lines round his neck and putting the finishing touches to the magnificence of his full dress.

"Nonsense, child! I must go with the regiment."

Nina sighed. She had now been three months with her father, and they did not seem to understand each other any better. She knew him to be a fine soldier, and that the regiment was proud of their Iron Colonel as a commanding officer. But underneath that hard, cold exterior she did so long to find a loving, tender parent. Her life was very dull at Dustypore, and somehow her thoughts constantly went back to the P. and O. and Jack Harrage.

The sound of the band playing "Church Bells" over on the parade ground warned her it was time for service. As she drove past Dolly's bungalow she saw that young officer getting on his pony to canter off to parade. Watching him in the gloom of the verandah, she fancied she descried a familiar figure, cigar in mouth. A thrill of delight passed over her, and I fancy she hardly attended as much to the service as she should have done. Anyhow, as she watched the "Crimsons" swing away from the church portico to the inspiriting strains of the band, her heart sang for joy that Christmas morning.

The anteroom of the Crimson Cuirassiers was as comfortable as it could be made by a varied collection of cretonne-covered wicker chairs, periodically smashed up on "big" nights. But it seemed paradise to Nina as she sat there before dinner, making conversation with the giggling wife of the Collector, and saw a scarlet-clad infantry officer enter with Dolly. The next minute, with her head in a whirl, she was being introduced to "My school chum, Captain Harrage."

A rush for dinner followed. The Colonel, with anything but an amiable expression, took in the Collector's wife, whose husband followed with Nina. He was a naturally dull little man, whose mind had become fossilised with twenty-five years of India. He devoted himself to the "Crimsons'" menu, leaving Nina plenty of leisure to listen to the chaff and laughter which emanated from either end of the long table, groaning under racing and presentation plate, where congregated the junior officers, and to catch constantly Jack Harrage's eye.

After dinner an awful interval of penance followed for Nina when alone with the ladies. Finally, she left them alone to discuss the maladies of infants and the petty larceny of domestics, and turned over a paper to collect her thoughts.

After what seemed an age, some of the younger men slipped in, leaving their seniors to smoke and talk.

"Let's have a ladies' pool," suggested some one, "love game."

"Come along, now, Mrs. Smith, darlin'," quoth the Vet., who had dined well, if not wisely, to the Quartermaster's wife, "it's a poor heart that never rejoices, and shure isn't it Christmas night?"

"Lor, Mr. McCartney," returned the lady, bridling, "but I never 'andled a cue in my life."

"Do come, Miss Heytesbury," whispered Dolly to Nina, "don't you see we must do *something*?"

They trooped into the billiard-room, where Nina was given a ball, and played in her turn after two or three times of asking, for she was deep in conversation with Jack Harrage by the open window.

"You seemed surprised to see me to-night."

"I fancied I saw you in Mr. Gray's verandah this morning. But I wasn't sure."

"Didn't I tell you I'd turn up? I couldn't get leave before. Do you mean to say you didn't trust me?"

"Green or blue, brown's your player," gabbled the native marker. Nina went up to the table and made a miss.

"There, Miss Heytesbury," remarked the major; "that's your last life. I regret to say you're defunct."

"I'm so glad," whispered Jack. "Come into the verandah; it's such a lovely night."

"Yes," said she, hardly knowing what she said "only much colder than those moonlight nights at sea. How moonlight disguises the place and makes it pretty!"

Harrage turned and looked her full in the face.

"Miss Heytesbury—Nina, you *do* remember those nights at sea? Oh! so often, especially that last evening, I was so nearly speaking to you, but it wouldn't have done. Now please listen, don't turn away, Nina! It's all altered, it's all right now; I've got my company; and more than that, my cousin's been killed—an accident—and I'm my uncle's heir. And I've come here to ask you—to tell you——"

He never finished, for he got his arm round her waist, and the next minute her head was on his shoulder, and he was kissing her.

"Miss Heytesbury! Miss Heytesbury!" said a voice at the window. "Mr. and Mrs. Brown want to say good night to you."

And Nina escaped back into the glaring room.

"I shall come and see the Colonel to-morrow morning," whispered Harrage, later, as he put on her cloak.

An hour or so after, Dolly and Jack were walking down the moonlit road to the former's bungalow.

"I say, old chappie," cried Dolly, breaking silence, "you needn't walk such a trot, it's close by. By-the-by," he added, "I hope you've not been awfully bored. But it being Christmas night, and women about, made it rather deadly."

"Deadly? My dear boy," cried Jack, throwing away the end of his cigar, "it's the jolliest——"

The jubilant expression of his friend's face and tone made Dolly stare. Then a sudden light seemed to break in upon him.

"Well, now I come to think of it, you have had rather the best of it with Miss Heytesbury. She's awfully pretty, but she's always down on me somehow," he added rather mournfully.

Just then the canter of a horse's hoof sounded behind them on the dusty side of the road, accompanied with shouts and chaff.

"It's only the omnibus," explained Dolly.

The "omnibus" was Benham's old grey Arab, which he rode to mess to save the polish of his boots, and which as many others as could sit behind habitually assisted him in riding back from mess.

The friends did not speak again till they found themselves in Dolly's room. It was very bare; its owner had about fifteen hundred a year of his own, but might only have had one to judge by its furniture, which consisted chiefly of boxes and saddles, rows of boots, and bunches of polo-sticks, with a small camp-bed in the centre.

As the only easy-chair was occupied by a sleeping terrier, Harrage sat down on the edge of the bed, and Dolly yelled to a slumbering bearer in the verandah till the latter produced some soda-water and tumblers. Dolly measured out the whisky, and then advanced, glass in hand, to his friend. But he paused.

"What's up, old chap? You look as if you'd turned up trumps!"

Jack jumped up and slapped his friend so vehemently on the back that he nearly made him spill the drink.

"And so I have, Doll, old man! Congratulate me! She is the——"

Dolly's mouth opened, and the drink had another narrow escape.

"She? What? Who? Miss Heytesbury? Oh, Gemini! what an ass I've been! Of course that's why you wanted to come and put up with me."

And he sat down dejectedly on the bed, and tossed off the potion himself to hide his mortification.

"I'm going to tackle the old un to-morrow morning," were Jack's last words as he turned in.

"Well, you'll find him a tough nut to crack," rejoined Dolly from his pillows. "No one has ever yet got to the soft side of him. Even she has not improved him as we thought she would."

* * * * *

After a late breakfast the Colonel sat next morning in the verandah smoking, in plain clothes. There was no parade or orderly-room, and he was not going near barracks; for even in such an admirable regiment as the Crimson Cuirassiers, Christmas comes but once a year, and the officers were so lavish in their troop dinners that the men needed a day to get over them.

Nina flitted above the verandah singing for very blitheness of heart, watering her plants, feeding her parrots. As he watched her, the Iron Colonel's face softened ever so little. Was she at last stealing into his long-frozen heart?

A horse came up the drive. Probably an orderly with papers to sign. But the old bearer brought a card on a waiter.

"Captain John Harrage."

All the softness instantly faded out of the Iron Colonel's face, giving place to a look of strong hatred as he glared blankly at the card. Then he looked up, and its owner stood before him.

Tall and handsome, but rather embarrassed, wishing the whole thing well over that he might go and look on Nina, Harrage could not for the life of him understand why the Colonel should look at him so alarmingly. But he knew he was a good match, he felt sure of Nina, and, not being naturally deficient in pluck, went boldly to work.

"I must apologise for coming so early, Colonel," he began, his uneasiness increasing, "but I couldn't rest any longer without speaking to you. I've come to tell you—to ask you—fact is, I've proposed to your daughter and I hope——"

The Colonel looked down again at the card, and then again at the young fellow. He rose slowly and stood back a few paces, and looked him all over from the top of his sun-helmet to the last button of his gaiter. Harrage returned the stare, thinking the Colonel indeed more difficult to get on with than he had anticipated for he was doubtless mad.

"Good God," faltered the elder man at last, "I could swear it was the same twenty years after!"

Jack thought he had better play his trump card.

"Perhaps you are unaware that recently, through the death of my cousin, I am, in position and prospects, no unworthy——"

The Colonel turned sharply upon him.

"Not another word! The less you say the less you'll have to regret. Listen!"

The look of hate was gone. He had resumed his habitual icy manner, but was evidently repressing violent emotions with a mighty effort.

"Listen!" he said, sitting down and motioning to Jack to do the same, but speaking with knitted brow and averted face, looking out into the compound.

"Twenty years ago I was in another regiment, the Scarlet Lancers."

"My father was a short time in them," murmured Jack.

Without, apparently, noticing the interruption the Colonel continued—

"I had not been married long. Nina was only two. I sent her and her mother up to the hills out of the heat. I did it for the best; I know I was not always tender to her, that I often neglected her; I blame myself for much; but this I did for the best. She was very young and inexperienced, and I asked a man in the regiment, a married man, with a wife and boy at home, my friend whom I trusted, to look after her, and, by God! he did. There was a great deal of talk; it came to my ears. I rushed up to the hill-station, madly jealous; I struck her! Then she left me, with *him* of course. He left the army; I exchanged. It was all over India at the time. Did you never hear of it?"

"Never," replied Jack, interested and astonished. "An awful business! But if it makes you afraid of marriage, for Nina, rest assured nothing of the kind shall ever——'

The Colonel rose from his chair, and looked fixedly at Harrage.

"Young man," he said, "the man who wrecked my life, who made me the hopeless, faithless wretch you see me, was your father!"

With that he turned on his heel and strode into the drawing-room to meet the white face of his child, who had overheard all and fell senseless at his feet.

* * * * *

"He's a d—d brute!" said Dolly to himself, as he came out of the Colonel's bungalow, nearly twelve months later, where Nina was lying on the sofa so weak and white after another attack of fever, that it made Dolly miserable to see her. "He's a d—d brute, and she's just breaking her heart about Harrage."

Of course Dolly was *au fait* with the unhappy termination of his friend's love-affair, though without knowing the reasons which led to it. A week later he met Jack Harrage at a down-country race meeting. The latter looked seedy.

"I'm just going to cut it all," he said. "My uncle wants me at home to look after things, and I'm sick of the service!"

Dolly opened his eyes, for he knew Jack used to consider soldiering the only thing worth living for.

Then Jack asked—

"Any news?"

Dolly knew what that meant, and told him Nina had been ill again, and added that she was leaving Dustypore for a week's change at Sirdhana, an old native palace hard by.

Knowing this, imagine Jack Harrage's horror, on returning to his regiment, to read in the first paper he took up:—

"FATAL ACCIDENT AT SIRDHANA.—An alarming carriage accident took place on Thursday at Sirdhana, where Miss Heytesbury, daughter of Colonel Heytesbury, of the Crimson Cuirassiers, had gone for change of air. The horses bolted in the carriage, the groom thrown out and killed, and the vehicle upset opposite the Roman Catholic convent, whither Miss Heytesbury was conveyed, and found to be suffering from concussion of the brain."

Jack went straight to his Colonel and asked for a few days' leave, looking so upset that it was granted without a word.

When Nina recovered consciousness twenty-four hours after her accident, she found herself lying in the room she had been occupying in the Sirdhana palace.

This was a large double-storied building, standing in a garden, which had been erected some hundred years before by a European adventurer who had married a powerful *begum* of those parts. She was a woman of strong character, who, being converted to Christianity, had built the Roman Catholic cathedral, convent, and schools close by. The Sirdhana palace, with its green groves and terrace, was a favourite resort with the European officers from Dustypore.

The room was large and lofty and fairly furnished.

Portraits of the grim *begum* and her French husband looked down upon Nina from the walls. The cathedral bells were ringing for vespers, and a European sister of mercy, in her conventional garb, sat by Nina's bed. She was a tall, thin, wan-looking woman, whose ascetic face, in its fearful grave-clothes headdress, looked probably older than it really was. But her expression was kind though sad, and it became almost transfigured with delight when she perceived that Nina was herself again. Kneeling down she covered the girl's hand with kisses, and then, closing her eyes, offered prayers of thanksgiving, while great tears rolled down her cheeks.

Then the doctors came in, and she disappeared. When Nina asked for her later, she was told that Sister Magdalen had overdone herself with penance and prayers, and had had one of her heart attacks.

However, next day she came back to Nina's bedside, and at the latter's earnest request took up her post there permanently. Something seemed to draw the poor heart-broken child to this sad woman, who seemed to have suffered too. In her, at last, she found the sympathy she so longed for.

Before the day was out, Nina was lying with her hand clasped in Sister Magdalen's, pouring into her sympathising ear all her sad story about Jack Harrage.

"I can't forget him, though I've tried to," she concluded. "And it does seem so terribly hard we should be separated like this through no fault of our own."

Sister Magdalen caught her breath sharply.

"Surely if my mother had ever thought of the misery her conduct would inflict on her child, she would have paused ere it was too late. But she could not have been good and loving as you are, sister," she added, looking up. " But why do you cry, dear sister?"

And she tried to draw down the wan face to her lips.

But Sister Magdalen quietly put her aside, and sinking on her knees by the bed covered her face with her hands.

"No, no, child, not that! I am not worthy, I am not good; no one is good. I am the most miserable of sinners!" And her lips moved in silent prayer. Then she hurriedly left the room.

A carriage drove up to the broad flight of steps, and a young man jumped out hastily and advanced eagerly towards Sister Magdalen with inquiries after Nina. She answered him at length, allaying the terrible anxiety which had devoured him on his journey ever since he had heard of the accident. Then she added—

"I fancy you must be Captain Harrage. To-morrow is Christmas Day; come over here again, and perhaps I may have good news for you."

The Colonel arrived late on Christmas Eve. He had been away on a distant court-martial at the time of his daughter's accident, and had now come as fast as duty and the train would allow him.

Till he heard how near he had been to losing her, I fancy he had hardly realised how much she was to him, and there was very little of the Iron Colonel left about him as he clasped her in his arm with his eyes full of tears.

The first thing on Christmas morning Nina begged him to go and look for the kind sister who had nursed her, and thank her himself.

He sought her in the cathedral—a white-washed building in pseudo-Gothic style, with a thin Italian campanile. The interior boasted a tawdry altar and the elaborate tombs of the *begum* and her husband.

High mass was being celebrated. A choir of native Christian boys were singing the "Gloria in Excelsis," while the sisters knelt around. The music was inferior, the surroundings tawdry, yet the Colonel felt strangely moved and softened as the divine Christmas greeting of "Peace on earth, good-will towards men," rang through the building.

Suddenly one of the sisters rose from her knees and came towards him standing at the door. Something in her walk and figure seemed to him like a memory of long ago, but her conventual dress was a complete disguise.

"You are Colonel Heytesbury," said the voice, which sounded strangely familiar. "Your child has been given back to you out of the very jaws of death. Do not stand between her and the man she loves. Make her happy."

The Colonel stared at her coldly and proudly. Then he recollected himself.

"If you are Sister Magdalen, I have come specially to thank you most heartily for all your kindness to my daughter. But I am really at a loss to understand why you should interfere in her private affairs," he added haughtily.

The sister laid her hand on his arm and looked up into his face.

"Why? Because I am her mother!"

Then she continued hurriedly, with downcast eyes—

"I know I have forfeited all my rights over her; I know I am not worthy that she should even guess who I am! I do not seek to palliate my crime, which, God knows, I have repented of with tears and penances these many years; I do not ask *you* to forgive me. But, Harold Heytesbury," she continued, sinking on her knees at his feet and pointing towards the altar, "as you hope for mercy above, I ask you to be merciful to those who have done you no harm!"

The Colonel walked into the church and sat down on the nearest seat to gain time. There was a fearful struggle in the man's heart between pride and love. But the choir sang out again that angelic message of forgiveness, and the woman waiting in the porch watched his face.

At last he rose and came slowly out. As he did so he ran against Jack Harrage coming up the steps.

The latter drew back, the Colonel hesitated a moment, and then held out his hand.

"Will you come out with me? I want to speak to you."

Sister Magdalen watched them moving together across the hot, glaring road to the palace, and then she slipped in by a back way and went to Nina's room.

"Have you seen my father? asked the latter. "He wanted to see you to thank you."

"He has done so amply," replied Sister Magdalen, coming up to Nina's sofa. Then she added—

"I think I have provided for you as happy a Christmas Day as you ever had."

"Happier than last year?" asked Nina, with a sigh.

"Far, as you will see. But kiss me first."

She knelt down, and Nina's fair young face kissed the worn one, which was lit up with a smile of deepest peace.

Then voices were heard approaching, and almost before Sister Magdalen had time to escape the Colonel led Jack Harrage into the room.

An hour later Nina was saying to the latter—

"Before you go back to-night, Jack, I must show you to the kind sister who nursed me, and who has heard all about you. Father, send and fetch her."

She was found kneeling as in prayer before the cathedral altar; but when they who came to fetch her touched her, they found the poor, suffering heart had stopped beating for ever.

IN DEATH THEY WERE NOT DIVIDED.

This was how it happened. In the very beginning it was all the fault of that sou'-west gale in the Channel and the Bay of Biscay which compelled her chaperon to take to her berth and stop there. Thus Beatrice Brundon, at the first few meals on board the good ship *Bunderbust*, had to chaperon herself; and he, Gregory Ayshford, subaltern of artillery, sat nearly opposite to her the first day at dinner. To eat with your plate in a fiddle, holding on the while with the other hand to the edge of the table, requires some adroitness. Overhead, in a swinging rack repose wine-glasses and bottles, which would otherwise infallibly start toboggan races up and down the table. He handed her the water; she looked up and thanked him with a smile, at the same time spilling half in her endeavour to fill her glass. This misadventure she attributed later, not entirely to a lurch the ship gave—Gregory's eyes fixed on her made her nervous.

By next day at dinner-time, the former had tipped the chief-steward, and managed that his place at table was shifted from the vicinity of a frowsy High Court Judge to Beatrice's side. When the chaperon recovered her appetite, and emerged once more into the outer world of the saloon, she found the pair chatting and laughing as if they had known each other all their lives.

But they were not entirely idle and frivolous on board ship, these two. By the time they reached Malta she had instructed him in the mysteries of *reversis;* and had, in return, been taught by him how to throw a rope quoit into a bucket with considerable precision. On balmy, starlit evenings on deck, when the sea was like oil, and the piano jingled under the awning, they discovered their waltz steps agreed admirably; while their delight in the long phosphorescent streak in the wake of the *Bunderbust* (to be seen best from a quiet corner behind the wheel-house) was mutual and intense. They bought lace together at Malta, and ostrich-feathers at Aden, and in both their peregrinations ashore at these places, unaccountably lost their chaperon.

What wonder that when the *Bunderbust* dropped anchor off the Apollo Bunder, in Bombay Harbour, each felt that the best part of their lives had come to an end. India loomed before them wide and vast. Should they ever meet again?

*   *   *   *   *

Mrs. Brundon sat in dim indolence in her bungalow, and wove matrimonial webs for the daughter she had not seen since she was six years old. Herself the wife of a great civilian functionary, ruling hundreds of thousands of dusky fellow-subjects in a district as large as an English county, and rolling in rupees and honours, Mrs. Brundon dreamed of a like position for her daughter. And when Beatrice made her appearance, almost a stranger, but as fair a specimen of Anglo-Saxon maidenhood as could be found between Peshawur and Galle, Mrs. Brundon promised to herself that she should make a great match.

The beautiful, but all too short, cold weather of India deepened into a fierce glaring spring, and the steady rise of the thermometer warned all who were able to do so to betake themselves to fresh woods and pastures new ere the merry month of May burst in all its fury over the sun-baked plains. Up among the ilexes and rhododendrons of Nynee Tal, where the giant crags of Cheena mirror themselves in the green willow-girdled lake, all was fresh, and cool, and bracing. Ferns carpeted ravine and dell, and fringed the gnarled trunks of the evergreen oaks. Rhododendrons dyed crimson patches on the mountain sides, and the notes of the *koel*—a fair imitation of the cuckoo—rang from the forest depths. But Beatrice's heart sighed with the poet—

> Ah, when in other climes we meet,
> Some vale or isle enchanting,
> Where all looks flow'ry, wild, and sweet,
> And naught save love is wanting;
> We think how great had been our bliss
> If heaven had but assigned us
> To live and die in scenes like this
> With some we've left behind us.

Not, however, that love was conspicuous by its absence at Nynee Tal. *Au contraire*, the naughty little god revels in such an earthly paradise. But it was not the sort of love Beatrice sighed for. Girls are so unreasonable! There was Mr. Cramwell, a rising young secretary to Government; Mr. Brydges, the clever engineer just appointed to a coveted post; Mr. Judge, the magistrate of Cutcheriabad; all literally pestering her with attentions. They would fain have filled her programme at dances with their united autographs;

they squabbled and sulked as to who should be her partner at tennis, her companion in her mountain rides. But she would have nothing to say to them. She could not forget the *Bunderbust* and Gregory Ayshford.

Mrs. Brundon first marvelled and then remonstrated when one after another eligible *parti* was dismissed. But she made no effort to understand the character or to elicit the confidence of the child so long parted from her by the cruel exigencies of an Indian life, and brought up among strangers. There are as good fish in the sea as ever came out of it; the child is young and can afford to wait, quoth the mother.

But the end of the season brought other fish to her net than Mrs. Brundon intended. Full of memories of the *Bunderbust* and the jolly voyage out, came Gregory Ayshford to Nynee Tal. The rains were over and gone; the monsoon of Beatrice's discontent was passed; and the world smiled once more green and fresh in the September sunshine. Fate, in the shape of an attack of fever, which opportunely prostrated Mrs. Brundon, favoured the lovers.

They rowed about the lake in the cool of the evenings, when the Tiger's Hill cast long shadows across the green water. They scaled together the mountain top in early morning on active hill ponies, and gazed on the wonderful white world of snow and ice, ere it became veiled in the rising haze of heat. Together they watched from Snow Seat a veritable transformation scene, repeated each evening when a wondrous sunset cast rosy reflections on the snow giants opposite.

And this was the end of it all—only this: A stiff, cold English lady seated in her verandah drawing-room, and calmly crushing the dearest hopes of the young man who stood appealingly before her. A young girl sobbing on her bed, while her lover rides away broken-hearted down the hill. Only this. But it was enough.

As if in pity at their fate, the heavens began to weep again. For three long days the monsoon burst out afresh, lashing the lake into fury, scarring the mountain side with watercourses, and goading the torrents into mad cascades. The world, the while, lay wrapped in fog, and the patter of rain on roof and tree ceased not.

When the skies lifted somewhat, a vague rumour of alarm spread through Nynee Tal. Undermined by rain and torrent, part of the steep hill-side had fallen, burying a house and some natives. A panic spread, and the news went round that the whole mountain side was unsafe.

Mrs. Brundon was out when Gregory galloped wildly up to the verandah whence he had been so ruthlessly expelled, and calling, all unmindful of the past, to Beatrice, by name, rushed into the house.

But, even as she came towards him, there was a cracking of joists and timbers and the structure reeled and shook. Instinctively Gregory caught Beatrice in his arms.

No human eye saw, no one this side of eternity will ever know, what happened next. A great cloud of dust, like that which of old veiled the destruction of Gomorrah, arose from the mountain side and mercifully hid the scene.

When it cleared away there was a great scar on the hill-side, and a vast pile of *débris* filled up the head of the valley. Beneath lay buried houses, temples, shops, soldiers, priests, natives, and, under that great funeral pile, lies to this day the nameless grave of Gregory and Beatrice.

FINIS.

September, 1890.

SELECTED LIST

OF

Illustrated and General Publications

BY

THACKER, SPINK & CO., CALCUTTA.

W. THACKER & CO., 87, NEWGATE ST., LONDON.

CAN ALSO BE OBTAINED OF
THACKER & CO., LIMITED, BOMBAY.

Lays of Ind. By ALIPH CHEEM. Comic, Satirical, and Descriptive Poems illustrative of Anglo-Indian Life. Seventh Edition. Enlarged. With 70 Illustrations. Cloth elegant, gilt edges. Rs. 7-8 (10s. 6d.)

"Aliph Cheem presents us in this volume with some highly amusing ballads and songs, which have already in a former edition warmed the hearts and cheered the lonely hours of many an Anglo-Indian, the pictures being chiefly those of Indian life. There is no mistaking the humour, and at times, indeed, the fun is both 'fast and furious.' One can readily imagine the merriment created round the camp fire by the recitation of 'The Two Thumpers,' which is irresistibly droll. . . . The edition before us is enlarged, and contains illustrations by the author, in addition to which it is beautifully printed and handsomely got up, all which recommendations are sure to make the name of Aliph Cheem more popular in India than ever."—*Liverpool Mercury.*

"The 'Lays' are not only Anglo-Indian in origin, but out-and-out Anglo-Indian in subject and colour. To one who knows something of life at an Indian 'station' they will be especially amusing. Their exuberant fun at the same time may well attract the attention of the ill-defined individual known as the 'general reader.'"—*Scotsman.*

"This is a remarkably bright little book. 'Aliph Cheem, supposed to be the *nom de plume* of an officer in the 18th Hussars, is, after his fashion, an Indian Bon Gaultier. In a few of the poems the jokes, turning on local names and customs, are somewhat esoteric; but taken throughout, the verses are characterised by high animal spirits, great cleverness, and most excellent fooling."—*World.*

"To many Anglo-Indians the lively verses of 'Aliph Cheem' must be very well known; while to those who have not yet become acquainted with them we can only say, read them on the first opportunity. To those not familiar with Indian life they may be specially commended for the picture which they give of many of its lighter incidents and conditions, and of several of its ordinary personages."—*Bath Chronicle.*

Departmental Ditties and other Verses. Being Humorous Poems of Indian Official Life. By RUDYARD KIPLING. Fifth Edition. In square 32mo. Rs. 3 (5s.)

"They reflect with light gaiety the thoughts and feelings of actual men and women, and are true as well as clever. . . . Mr. Kipling achieves the feat of making Anglo-Indian society flirt and intrigue visibly before our eyes. . . . His book gives hope of a new literary star of no mean magnitude rising in the east."—*Sir W. W. Hunter in The Academy.*

"As for that terrible, scathing piece, 'The Story of Uriah,' we know of nothing with which to compare it, and one cannot help the wretched feeling that it is true. . . . 'In Spring Time' is the most pathetic lament of an exile we know in modern poetry."—*Graphic.*

Denizens of the Jungles; a series of Sketches of Wild Animals, illustrating their form and natural attitude. With letterpress description of each plate. By R. A. STERNDALE, F.R.G.S., F.Z.S. Author of "Natural History of the Mammalia of India," "Seonee," &c. Oblong folio. Rs. 10 (16s.)

I.—Aborigines and Game.
II.—Tiger.
III.—Panther and Monkeys.
IV.—Black Bears.
V.—Tiger and Elephant.
VI.—Wild Boar and Tiger.
VII.—Blue Bull and Wild Dogs.
VIII.—Gaur.
IX.—Buffalo and Rhinoceros.
X.—Spotted Deer and Leopard.
XI.—Sambur.
XII.—Marco Polo's Sheep.

Useful Hints to Young Shikaris on the Gun and Rifle. By "THE LITTLE OLD BEAR." Reprinted from the *Asian.* Crown 8vo. Rs. 2-8.

A Natural History of the Mammalia of India, Burmah and Ceylon. By R. A. STERNDALE, F.R.G.S., F.Z.S., &c., Author of "Seonee," "The Denizens of the Jungle," "The Afghan Knife," &c. With 170 Illustrations by the Author and Others. In Imperial 16mo. Uniform with "Riding," "Hindu Mythology," and "Indian Ferns." Rs. 10 (12s. 6d.)

"It is the very model of what a popular natural history should be."—*Knowledge.*

"An amusing work with good illustrations."—*Nature.*

"Full of accurate observation, brightly told."—*Saturday Review.*

"The results of a close and sympathetic observation."—*Athenæum.*

"The notices of each animal are, as a rule, short, though on some of the larger mammals—the lion, tiger, pard, boar, &c.—ample and interesting details are given, including occasional anecdotes of adventure. The book will, no doubt, be specially useful to the sportsman, and, indeed, has been extended so as to include all territories likely to be reached by the sportsman from India. . . . Those who desire to obtain some general information, popularly conveyed, on the subject with which the book deals, will, we believe, find it useful."—*The Times.*

"Has contrived to hit a happy mean between the stiff scientific treatise and the bosh of what may be called anecdotal zoology."—*The Daily News.*

Kurrachee: Its Past, Present and Future. By A. F. BAILLIE, F.R.G.S. With Maps, Plans, and Photographs. Super royal 8vo. Rs. 15-12.

Riding : On the Flat and Across Country. A Guide to Practical Horsemanship. By Capt. M. H. HAYES. Illustrated by Sturgess. Third Edition. Revised and Enlarged. Imperial 16mo. [*In the press.*

"Mr. Hayes has supplemented his own experience on race-riding by resorting to Tom Cannon, Fordham, and other well-known jockeys for illustration. 'The Guide' is, on the whole, thoroughly reliable; and both the illustrations and the printing do credit to the publishers."—*Field.*

"It has, however, been reserved for Captain Hayes to write what in our opinion will be generally accepted as the most comprehensive, enlightened, and 'all round' work on riding, bringing to bear as he does not only his own great experience, but the advice and practice of many of the best recognised horsemen of the period."—*Sporting Life.*

"Captain Hayes is not only a master of his subject, but he knows how to aid others in gaining such a mastery as may be obtained by the study of a book."—*The Standard.*

The Points of the Horse. A Familiar Treatise on Equine Conformation. By Capt. M. H. HAYES. Illustrated by J. H. OSWALD BROWN. *In preparation.*

Describes the points in which the perfection of each class of horses consists; illustrated by very numerous reproductions of Photographs of Living Typical Animals.

The Horsewoman. By Capt. M. H. HAYES and Mrs. HAYES. Numerous Illustrations. [*In the press.*

Hayes' Sporting News. A Weekly Journal of Racing, Amusements, Natural History, &c. Edited by Capt. M. H. HAYES. Annual Subscription, Rs. 16.

Fourth Edition, revised, with additional Illustrations. (*In the press.*)

Veterinary Notes for Horse-Owners.—A Hand Book of Veterinary Medicine and Surgery, written in popular language. By Captain M. HORACE HAYES, M.R.C.V.S.

"The work is written in a clear and practical way."—*Saturday Review.*

"Of the many popular veterinary books which have come under our notice, this is certainly one of the most scientific and reliable."—*The Field.*

"We heartily welcome the second edition of this exceedingly useful book. The first edition was brought out about two years since, but the work now under notice is fully double the size of its predecessor, and, as a matter of course, contains more information."—*The Sporting Life.*

"Captain Hayes, in the new edition of 'Veterinary Notes,' has added considerably to its value by including matter which was omitted in the former editions, and rendered the book, if larger, at any rate more useful to those non-professional people who may be inclined or compelled to treat their own horses when sick or injured. So far as we are able to judge, the book leaves nothing to be desired on the score of lucidity and comprehensiveness."---*Veterinary Journal.*

Illustrated Horse Breaking.—By Capt. M. H. HAYES. Numerous Illustrations by J. H. OSWALD BROWN. In Small 4to. uniform with "Riding." Rs. 16 (21s.)

1. Theory of Horse Breaking. 2. Principles of Mounting. 3. Horse Control. 4. Rendering Docile. 5. Giving Good Mouths. 6. Teaching to Jump. 7. Mount for First Time. 8. Breaking for Ladies' Riding. 9. Breaking to Harness. 10. Faults of Mouth. 11. Nervousness and Impatience. 12. Jibbing. 13. Jumping Faults. 14. Faults in Harness. 15. Aggressiveness. 16. Riding and Driving Newly-broken Horse. 17. Stable Vices.

"Far and away the best reasoned-out book on Breaking under a new system we have seen."—*Field.*

"Clearly explained in simple, practical language, made all the more clear by a set of capital drawings."—*Scotsman.*

Training and Horse Management in India. By Captain M. HORACE HAYES, author of "Veterinary Notes for Horse Owners," "Riding," &c. Third Edition. Crown 8vo. Rs. 5 (8s. 6d.)

"No better guide could be placed in the hands of either amateur horseman or veterinary surgeon."—*The Veterinary Journal.*

"A useful guide in regard to horses anywhere. . . . . . Concise, practical, and portable."—*Saturday Review.*

Soundness and Age of Horses. With one hundred illustrations. A Complete Guide to all those features which require attention when purchasing Horses, distinguishing mere defects from the symptoms of unsoundness, with explicit instructions how to conduct an examination of the various parts. By Capt. M. H. HAYES. Post 8vo. Rs. 6 (8s. 6d.)

"A very concise and comprehensive veterinary and legal guide."—*Army and Navy Magazine.*

"A capital little volume, admirably illustrated, replete with sound legal knowledge made perfectly clear to the mind of the layman. It is a book for cavalry officers and hunting men."—*Broad Arrow.*

The Student's Manual of Tactics. By Capt. M. HORACE HAYES. Specially written for the use of candidates preparing for the Militia, Military Competitive Examinations, and for promotion. Crown 8vo. Rs. 4-4 (6s.)

"There is no better Manual on Tactics than the one which Captain Hayes has written."—*Naval and Military Gazette.*

"'The Student's Manual of Tactics' is an excellent book. Principles are reasoned out, and details explained in such a way that the student cannot fail to get a good grasp of the subject. Having served in both the artillery and infantry, and being a practical writer, as well as 'a coach,' the author of this manual had exceptional qualifications for the task he has accomplished."—*Broad Arrow.*

Indian Racing Reminiscences. Being Entertaining Narratives and Anecdotes of Men, Horses, and Sport. By Captain M. HORACE HAYES, Author of "Veterinary Notes," "Training and Horse Management," &c. Illustrated with 22 Portraits and 20 Engravings. Imperial 16mo. Rs. 6 (8s. 6d.)

Medical Jurisprudence for India. By I. B. LYON, C.I.E., F.C.S., Brigade-Surgeon, Professor of Chemistry and Medical Jurisprudence, Grant Medical College, Bombay. Revised as to the Legal Matter by J. D. Inverarity, Barrister-at-Law. Illustrated. Second Edition. Rs. 16 (25s.)

"The treatise on 'Medical Jurisprudence for India' by Dr. Lyon is an excellent text-book for students, and a useful book of reference for practitioners. The subject is exhaustively treated, the information is concisely put, and there is a pleasing absence of 'padding.' The illustrations are among the most beautiful and accurate that we have seen in a book of this kind. The trustworthiness of the legal matter has been ensured by its submission to the revision of an able barrister."—*Saturday Review.*

"An admirable exposition of the Science of Medical Jurisprudence generally, but its special value lies in the fact that it has been written for the purpose of guidance for medical men practising in India . . . . . The book reflects great credit on the author and publishers. The letterpress is excellent—large bold type, and the illustrations are accurate representations of the originals. The diction is clear and concise, and is well worthy the author's reputation."—*The Lancet.*

Plain Tales from the Hills: A Collection of Stories. By RUDYARD KIPLING, Author of "Departmental Ditties and other Verses." Third Edition. Crown 8vo, cloth. Rs. 4-4 (6s.)

The Emperor Akbar: A Contribution towards the History of India in the XVI. Century. By FRID. AUGUSTUS, Count of Noer. Translated by Annette S. Beveridge. Two vols. 8vo. Rs. 8.

Hindu Mythology: Vedic and Puranic. By Rev. W. J. WILKINS, of the London Missionary Society, Calcutta. Illustrated by very numerous Engravings from Drawings by Native Artists. Uniform with "Lays of Ind," "Riding," &c. Rs. 7-8 (10s. 6d.)

"Mr. Wilkins has done his work well, with an honest desire to state facts apart from all theological prepossession, and his volume is likely to be a useful book of reference."—*Guardian.*

"In Mr. Wilkins's book we have an illustrated manual, the study of which will lay a solid foundation for more advanced knowledge, while it will furnish those who may have the desire without having the time or opportunity to go further into the subject, with a really extensive stock of accurate information."—*Indian Daily News.*

Echoes from Old Calcutta: being chiefly Reminiscences of the days of Warren Hastings, Francis, and Impey. By H. E. BUSTEED. Second Edition. Considerably Enlarged and Illustrated. Rs. 6 (8s. 6d.)

"Dr. Busteed has made an eminently readable, entertaining, and by no means uninstructive volume; there is not a dull page in the whole book." —*Saturday Review.*

"The book will be read by all interested in India"—*Army and Navy Magazine.*

"The papers deal with some of the most interesting episodes in the political and social history of Calcutta, and while some fresh light is thrown on all of them, more than one of them are placed in an entirely new aspect."—*Calcutta Review.*

"The story of that frail East Indian beauty, who became Princess of Benevento, has never been told in detail before, and Dr. Busteed could scarcely have found a livelier or more picturesque subject to illustrate Anglo-Indian life a hundred years ago."—*Times of India.*

"Not only can no one who reads these papers fail to appreciate either their interest or their literary merit, but it is only necessary to compare them with what has been previously published on the same subjects, to see that they form a contribution of no mean value to the history of the times with which they deal."—*The Englishman.*

Life and Teaching of Keshub Chunder Sen. By P. C. MAZUMDAR. Second and Cheaper Edition.

Indian Notes about Dogs: their Diseases and Treatment. By Major C——. Third Edition, Revised. Fcap. 8vo., cloth. Re. 1-8.

Indian Horse Notes: an Epitome of useful Information arranged for ready reference on Emergencies, and specially adapted for Officers and Mofussil Residents. All Technical Terms explained and Simplest Remedies selected. By Major C——, Author of "Indian Notes about Dogs." Second Edition, Revised and considerably Enlarged. Fcap. 8vo., cloth. Rs. 2.

Horse Breeding in India: being a Second Edition of "The Steeple Chase Horse; how to select, train, and ride him, with Notes on Accidents, Diseases, and their Treatment." By Major J. HUMFREY. Crown 8vo. Rs. 3-8.

Amateur Gardener in the Hills, Hints from various Authorities, adapted to the Hills. By AN AMATEUR. Crown 8vo. Rs. 2-8.

Eighth Edition. Crown 8vo. Rs. 7. (10s. 6d.)

The Management and Medical Treatment of
Children in India. By EDWARD A. BIRCH, M.D., Surgeon-Major Bengal Establishment. Second Edition, Revised. Being the Eighth Edition of "Goodeve's Hints for the Management of Children in India."

Dr. Goodeve.—"I have no hesitation in saying that the present edition is for many reasons superior to its predecessors. It is written very carefully, and with much knowledge and experience on the author's part, whilst it possesses the great advantage of bringing up the subject to the present level of Medical Science."

The Medical Times and Gazette, in an article upon this work and Moore's "Family Medicine for India," says:—"The two works before us are in themselves probably about the best examples of medical works written for non-professional readers. The style of each is simple, and as free as possible from technical expressions. The modes of treatment recommended are generally those most likely to yield good results in the hands of laymen; and throughout each volume the important fact is kept constantly before the mind of the reader, that the volume he is using is but a poor substitute for personal professional advice, for which it must be discarded whenever there is the opportunity."

A Tea Planter's Life in Assam.
By GEORGE M. BARKER. With Seventy-five Illustrations by the Author. Crown 8vo. Rs. 5-8 (7s. 6d.)

"Mr. Barker has supplied us with a very good and readable description, accompanied by numerous illustrations drawn by himself. What may be called the business parts of the book are of most value."—*Contemporary Review.*

"A very interesting and amusing book, artistically illustrated from sketches drawn by the Author."—*Mark Lane Express.*

A Complete List of Indian Tea Gardens, Indigo
Concerns, Silk Filatures, Sugar Factories, Cinchona Concerns, and Coffee Estates. With their Capital, Directors, Proprietors, Agents, Managers, Assistants, &c., and their Factory Marks by which the chests may be identified in the market. 5s.

"The strong point of the book is the reproduction of the factory marks, which are presented side by side with the letterpress. To buyers of tea and other Indian products on this side, the work needs no recommendation."—*British Trade Journal.*

The Tea Estates of Ceylon, their Acreage and
Proprietors. 1s. 6d., or with the "Indian Tea Gardens," 6s.

The Fauna of British India, including Ceylon and Burma. Published under the authority of the Secretary of State for India. Edited by W. T. Blanford, F.R.S., and Illustrated.
> MAMMALS described by W. T. Blanford. One volume. Parts I and II., Rs. 7-8 each.
> REPTILES and BATRACHIANS by A. Boulenger of the British Museum. Rs. 15.
> FISHES.—By F. Day, C.I.E., Deputy Surgeon-General. Two volumes. Rs. 15 each.
> BIRDS.—Three volumes.

Grasses.—Illustrations of some of the Grasses of the Southern Punjab. Being Photo-Lithographs of some of the principal Grasses found at Hissar. With short descriptive Letterpress, by William Coldstream, B.A., B.C.S., Fellow of the Punjab University and Member of the Royal Botanical Society of Edinburgh. Demy folio, Thirty-nine Plates beautifully executed by the University Press. Edinburgh. Rs. 16 (25s.)

Our Administration of India: being a complete Account of the Revenue and Collectorate Administration in all Departments, with special reference to the Work and Duties of a District Officer in Bengal. By H. A. D. PHILLIPS. Rs. 4-4 (6s.)

"In eleven chapters Mr. Phillips gives a complete epitome of the civil, in distinction from the criminal, duties of an Indian Collector. The information is all derived from personal experience. A polemical interest runs through the book, but this does not detract from the value of the very complete collections of facts and statistics given."—*London Quarterly Review.*

"It contains much information in a convenient form for English readers who wish to study the working of our system in the country districts of India."—*Westminster Review.*

"A very handy and useful book of information upon a very momentous subject, about which Englishmen know very little."—*Pall Mall Gazette.*

The Reconnoitrer's Guide and Field Book adapted for India. By Lieut.-Col. M. J. KING-HARMAN, B.S.C. Second Edition, Revised and Enlarged. In roan. Rs. 4.

It contains all that is required for the guidance of the Military Reconnoitrer in India: it can be used as an ordinary Pocket Note Book, or as a Field Message Book; the pages are ruled as a Field Book, and in sections, for written description or sketch.

"To officers serving in India this guide will be invaluable."—*Broad Arrow.*

The Culture and Manufacture of Indigo, with a Description of a Planter's Life and Resources. By WALTER MACLAGAN REID. Crown 8vo. With nineteen full-page Illustrations. Rs. 5 (7s. 6d.)

"It is proposed in the following Sketches of Indigo Life in Tirhoot and Lower Bengal to give those who have never witnessed the manufacture of Indigo, or seen an Indigo Factory in this country, an idea of how the finished marketable article is produced: together with other phases and incidents of an Indigo Planter's life, such as may be interesting and amusing to friends at home."—*Introduction.*

History of Civilization in Ancient India. Based on Sanscrit Literature. By ROMESH CHUNDER DUTT. Vol. 1. Vedic and Epic Ages, with Map. Vol. 2. Rationalistic Age. Vol. 3. Puranic Age. Crown 8vo. Each Rs. 4.

The Government of India. A primer for Indian Schools. By H. B. Second Edition. Sewed As. 8. Cloth Rs. 1.

Bombay Sketches. In Bengali. By S. TAGORE, Bo. C.S. With Photographic Illustrations. Royal 8vo. Rs. 8.

Tales from Indian History: being the Annals of India retold in Narratives. By J. TALBOYS WHEELER. Sixth Edition. Crown 8vo., cloth gilt. Rs. 2-8 (3s. 6d.)

"No young reader who revolts at the ordinary history presented to him in his school books will hesitate to take up this. No one can read a volume such as this without being deeply interested."—*Scotsman.*

"While the work has been written for them (natives), it has also been written for the people of England, who will find in the volume, perhaps for the first time, the history of our great dependency made extremely attractive reading."—*Saturday Review.*

Calcutta Turf Club: Rules of Racing, together with the Rules relating to Lotteries, Betting and Defaulters, and the Rules of the Calcutta Turf Club. *Authorised Edition.* (Revised on June 11, 1889). Cloth. Rs. 2.

Calcutta Turf Club: Racing Calendar. Vol. 1, August 1, 1888, to April 30, 1889. Rs. 4. Vol. 2, May 1, 1889, to April 30, 1890. Each Rs. 4.

Cæsar de Souza, Earl of Wakefield. By the Author of "India in 1983." Crown 8vo. Cloth. Rs. 2-8.

Leviora: being the Rhymes of a Successful Competitor. By T. F. BIGNOLD, Bengal Civil Service. 8vo. Rs. 7-8.

India in 1983. A Reprint of this celebrated brochure written at the time of the "Ilbert Bill." Fcap. 8vo. Re. 1.

UNDER PATRONAGE OF THE SECRETARY OF STATE.

Statistics of Hydraulic Works, and Hydrology
of England, Canada, Egypt, and India. Collected and reduced by LOWIS D'A. JACKSON, C.E., Author of "Canal and Culvert Tables," "Hydraulic Manual," "Aid to Engineering Solution," &c. Royal 8vo. Rs. 10 (15s.)

". . . Though apparently compiled primarily for the benefit of the India Public Works' Department, the book contains much information which is not generally known in England even amongst engineers, especially as regards the gigantic scale on which hydraulic works are carried out in foreign countries."—*The Builder.*

Game, Shore, and Water Birds of India.
By Col. A. LE MESSURIER, R.E., with 111 Illustrations. A *vade mecum* for Sportsmen. Embracing all the Birds at all likely to be met with in a Shooting Excursion. 8vo. Rs. 10 (15s.)

"To the man who cares for bird shooting, and the excellent sport which is almost illimitable on the lakes or 'tanks' in the Carnatic or the Deccan, Colonel Le Messurier's present work will be a source of great delight, as every ornithologic detail is given, in conjunction with the most artistic and exquisite drawings. . . . No sportsman's outfit for Upper India can be considered complete without this admirable work of reference."
—*Broad Arrow.*

A Manual of Surveying for India,
detailing the mode of operations on the Trigonometrical, Topographical and Revenue Surveys of India. Compiled by Sir H. L. THUILLIER, K.C.S.I., and Lieut.-Col. R. SMYTH. Prepared for the use of the Survey Department, and published under the authority of the Government of India. Royal 8vo. Rs. 16 (30s.)

The Hindoos as they are:
a description of the Manners, Customs, and Inner Life of Hindoo Society. Bengal. By SHIB CHUNDER BOSE. Second Edition. Revised. Crown 8vo. Rs. 5. (7s. 6d.)

"Lifts the veil from the inner domestic life of his countrymen."—*Westminster Review.*

A Memoir of the late Justice Onoocool Chunder Mookerjee.
By M. MOOKERJEE. Third Edition. 12mo. Re. 1 (2s. 6d.)

The Biography of a Native Judge, by a native, forming a most interesting and amusing illustration of Indian English.

"The reader is earnestly advised to procure the life of this gentleman, written by his nephew, and read it."—*The Tribes on my Frontier.*

Hints on the Study of English. By F. J. ROWE, M.A., and W. T. WEBB, M.A., Professors of English Literature, Presidency College, Calcutta. New Edition, Revised. Crown 8vo., cloth. Rs. 2-8.

A Companion Reader to "Hints on the Study of English." (Eighteenth Thousand.) Demy 8vo. Price Re. 1-4.

Talim-i-Zaban-i-Urdu. A Guide to Hindustani. By Dr. G. S. A. RANKING. Crown 8vo. Rs. 5.

Hidyat-al-Hukuma: A Guide to Medical Officers and Members of the Indian Service. By Dr. G. S. A. RANKING. Sewed. Re. 1-4.

Essays on Mohammadan Social Reform. By DELAWARR HOSAEN AHMED MEERZA. 2 vols. 8vo. Rs. 3.

Fifty Graduated Weekly Papers in Arithmetic, Algebra, and Geometry for the use of Students preparing for the Entrance Examinations of the Indian Universities. With Hints on Methods of Shortening Work and on the Writing of Examination Papers. By W. H. WOOD, B.A., F.C.S., Lecturer in Mathematics and Science, La Martiniere College. Re. 1-8.

Indian Lyrics. By W. TREGO WEBB, M.A., Bengal Education Service. Square 8vo., cloth gilt. Rs. 4 (7s. 6d.)

"He presents the various sorts and conditions of humanity that comprise the round of life in Bengal in a series of vivid vignettes. . . . . He writes with scholarly directness and finish."—*Saturday Review.*

"A pleasant book to read."—*Suffolk Chronicle.*

"The style is pretty pleasant, and the verses run smooth and melodious."—*Indian Mail.*

Hindustani as it ought to be Spoken. A Manual with Explanations, Vocabularies, and Exercises. By J. TWEEDIE, C.S. Rs. 2-8 (5s.).

Fishing in the Kumaon Lakes. By W. WALKER, M.D., M.A., Deputy Surgeon-General, N. W. P. With Map of the District and Plans of each Lake. Rs. 4.

Banting in India, with some Remarks on Diet and Things in General. By Surgeon-Major JOSHUA DUKE. Third Edition. Cloth. Re. 1-8.

Landholding; and the Relation of Landlord and Tenant in Various Countries of the World. By C. D. FIELD, M.A., LL.D. 8vo., cloth. Rs. 16.

"At once an able and skilled authority."—*The Field.*

"Supplies a want much felt by the leading public men in Bengal."— *Friend of India and Statesman.*

Queries at a Mess Table. What shall we Eat? What shall we Drink? By Surgeon-Major JOSHUA DUKE. Fcap. 8vo., cloth, gilt. Rs. 2-4.

Culinary Jottings. A Treatise in Thirty Chapters, on Reformed Cookery for Anglo-Indian Exiles. Based upon Modern English and Continental principles. With thirty Menus of Little Dinners worked out in detail, and an Essay on our kitchens in India. By "WYVERN." 8vo., cloth. Rs. 5-8.

Sweet Dishes. A Supplement to "Culinary Jottings." By "WYVERN." 8vo., cloth. Rs. 3-8.

A Text-Book of Indian Botany, Morphological, Physiological, and Systematic. Profusely Illustrated. By W. H. GREGG, B.M.S., Lecturer on Botany at the Hugli Government College. Cr. 8vo. Rs. 5; interleaved, Rs. 5-8.

Light and Shade. By HERBERT SHERRING. A Collection of Tales and Poems. Crown 8vo. Rs. 3.

A Romance of Thakote, and Other Tales. By F. C. C. Crown 8vo. Rs. 1.

Ashes for Bread: A Romance. By B. HARRINGTON. Crown 8vo. Re. 1-8.

Manual of Agriculture for India. By Lt. FREDERICK POGSON. Illustrated. Crown 8vo., cloth, gilt. Rs. 5 (7s. 6d.)

CONTENTS.—Origin and general character of soils—Ploughing and Preparing the ground for sowing seed—Manures and Composts—Wheat cultivation — Barley — Oats — Rye — Rice — Maize — Sugar - producing Sorghums—Common, or non-sugar-producing Sorghums—Sugar-cane Crops —Oil-seed Crops—Field Pea, Japan Pea, and Bean Crops—Dall, or Pulse Crops—Root Crops—Cold Spice Crops—Fodder Plants—Water-nut Crops —Ground-nut Crops—The Rush-nut, *vel* Chufas—Cotton Crops—Tobacco Crops—Mensuration—Appendix.

Roxburgh's Flora Indica; or, Description of Indian Plants. Reprinted literatim from Cary's Edition. 8vo., cloth. Rs. 5 (10s. 6d.)

The Future of the Date Palm in India. (Phœnix Dactylifera.) By E. BONAVIA, M.D., Brigade-Surgeon, Indian Medical Department. Crown 8vo., cloth. Rs. 2-8.

Kashgaria (Eastern or Chinese Turkestan), Historical, Geographical, Military, and Industrial. By Col. KUROPATKIN, Russian Army. Translated by Major GOWAN, H.M.'s Indian Army. 8vo. Rs. 6-8. (10s. 6d.)

Mandalay to Momien: a Narrative of the Two Expeditions to Western China of 1868 and 1875, under Cols. E. B. Sladen and H. Browne. Three Maps, numerous Views and Wood-cuts. By JOHN M. D. ANDERSON. Thick demy 8vo., cloth. Rs. 5. [1876.

British Burma and its People: being Sketches of Native Manners, Customs, and Religion. By Capt. C. J. F. S. FORBES. 8vo., cloth. Rs. 4-8. [1878.

Myam-Ma: The Home of the Burman. By TSAYA (Rev. H. POWELL). Crown 8vo. Rs. 2. [1886.

A Critical Exposition of the Popular "Jihad," showing that all the Wars of Mohammad were defensive, and that Aggressive War or Compulsory Conversion is not allowed in the Koran, &c. By Moulavi CHERAGH ALI, Author of "Reforms under Moslem Rule," "Hyderabad under Sir Salar Jung." 8vo. Rs. 6.

Ancient India as described by Ptolemy: Being a Translation of the Chapters on India and on Central and Eastern Asia in the Treatise on Geography by Klaudios Ptolemaios, the celebrated Astronomer : with Introduction, Commentary, Map of India according to Ptolemy, and a very copious Index. By J. W. McCRINDLE, M.A. 8vo., cloth, lettered. Rs. 4-4.

The Life of H.M. Queen Victoria, Empress of India. By JOHN J. POOL, Editor, "Indian Missionary.' With an Original Portrait from a Wax Medallion by Signor C. Moscatti, Assistant Engraver, Her Majesty's Mint, Calcutta. Crown 8vo. Paper, Re. 1. Cloth, Re. 1-4.

Poppied Sleep. By Mrs. H. A. FLETCHER, Author of "Here's Rue for You." Crown 8vo. Re. 1-8.

The Bengal Medical Service, April, 1885. Compiled by G. F. A. HARRIS, Surgeon, Bengal Medical Service. Royal 8vo. Rs. 2.

A Gradation List giving Medical and Surgical Degrees and Diplomas, and Universities, Colleges, Hospitals, and War Services, etc., etc.

Ague; or Intermittent Fever. By M. D. O'CONNELL, M.D. 8vo., sewed. Rs. 2.

Book of Indian Eras.—With Tables for calculating Indian Dates. By ALEXANDER CUNNINGHAM, C.S.I., C.I.E, Major-Genl., R.E., Bengal. Royal 8vo., cloth. Rs. 12.

Protestant Missions.—The Fourth Decennial Statistical Tables of Protestant Missions in India, Ceylon, and Burmah. Prepared, on information collected at the close of 1881, at the request of the Calcutta Missionary Conference, and with the concurrence of the Madras and Bombay Missionary Conferences. Super-Royal 8vo. Rs. 2-8.

A Map of the Civil Divisions in India, including Governments, Divisions, and Districts, Political Agencies and Native States. Folded. Re. 1.

The Landmarks of Snake Poison Literature. By VINCENT RICHARDS, F.R.C.S. Crown 8vo. Second Edition. Rs. 2-8.

Thacker's Guide to Calcutta: with **Chapters on** its Byepaths, &c., with Map. Fcap. 8vo.

Calcutta to Liverpool by China, Japan, and America, in 1877. By Lieut.-General Sir HENRY NORMAN. Second Edition. Fcap. 8vo., cloth. Rs. 2-8. (3s. 6d.)

The only book published on this interesting route between India and England.

Guide to Masuri, Landaur, Dehra Dun, and the Hills North of Dehra; including Routes to the Snows and other places of note; with Chapters on Garhwal (Tehri), Hardwar, Rurki, and Chakrata. By JOHN NORTHAM. Rs. 2-8.

A Handbook for Visitors to Agra and its Neighbourhood. By H. G. KEENE, C.S. Fourth Edition. Revised. Maps, Plans, &c. Fcap. 8vo., cloth. Rs. 2-8.

A Handbook for Visitors to Delhi and its Neighbourhood. By H. G. KEENE, C.S. Third Edition. Maps. Fcap. 8vo., cloth. Rs. 2-8.

A Handbook for Visitors to Allahabad, Cawnpore, and Lucknow. By H. G. KEENE, C.S. Second Edition, re-written and enlarged. Fcap. 8vo. (Reprinting).

Hills beyond Simla. Three Months' Tour from Simla, through Bussahir, Kunowar, and Spiti, to Lahoul. ("In the Footsteps of the Few.") By Mrs. J. C. MURRAY-AYNSLEY. Crown 8vo, cloth. Rs. 3.

A Romance of Thakote and other Tales. By F. C. C. Crown 8vo. Sewed. Re. 1.

Son Gruel; or, What he met i' the Mofussil (after two Noble Lords). Cantos I. and II. Fcap. 8vo. Re. 1 each.

An Historical Account of the Calcutta Collectorate. From the days of the Zemindars to the present time. By R. C. STERNDALE, author of "Municipal Work in India." 8vo., cloth. Rs. 2.

Life An Explanation of it. By W. SEDGWICK, Major, R.E. Crown 8vo., cloth. Rs. 2.

Elementary Statics and Dynamics. By W. N. BOUTFLOWER, B.A., late Scholar of St. John's College, Cambridge, and Professor of Mathematics, Muir Central College, Allahabad. Second Edition. Crown 8vo. Rs. 3-8.

Ince's Guide to Kashmir. Revised and Re-written. By Surgeon-Major JOSHUA DUKE. With Maps. Rs. 6.

A Key to the Entrance Course, 1891. (Calcutta University Entrance Examination, 1891.) By W. T. WEBB, M.A. Fcap. 8vo. Rs. 2.

Indian-English and Indian Character. By ELLIS UNDERWOOD. Fcap 8vo. Re. 1.

The Trial of Maharaja Nanda Kumar. A Narrative of a Judicial Murder. By H. BEVERIDGE, C.S. 8vo., cloth. Rs. 5.

The Indian Tribute and the Loss by Exchange. The failure of Bimetallism as a remedy for India's growing burden. By T. I. POLLARD, author of "Gold and Silver Weighed in the Balance." Crown 8vo., cloth. Rs. 2-8.

Gold and Silver Weighed in the Balance: A measure of their value, &c. By T. I. POLLARD, author of "The Indian Tribute, &c." Crown 8vo., cloth. Rs. 2-8.

Seonee: or, Camp Life on the Satpura Range. A Tale of Indian Adventure. By R. A. STERNDALE, Author of "Mammalia of India," "Denizens of the Jungles." Illustrated by the Author. With an Appendix. Second and cheaper edition post 8vo. Rs. 6 (8s. 6d.)

"He has strung these detached reminiscences together after a new plan, and has varied them with descriptions of Indian life, native and Anglo-Indian, which are very pleasant reading."—*Home News.*
"Mr. Sterndale's interesting narrative of Indian life."—*Broad Arrow.*

Modern Hinduism: Being an Account of the Religion and Life of the Hindus in Northern India. By W. J. WILKINS, of the London Missionary Society, Author of "Hindu Mythology, Vedic and Puranic." Demy 8vo. Price Rs. 8.

The Sepoy Officers' Manual. Second Edition. Revised. By Capt. E. G. BARROW. Rs. 2-8.

The Laws of Wealth: A Primer on Political Economy for the Middle Classes of India. By HORACE BELL, C.E. Fcap. 8 annas.

Reminiscences of Behar. By an Old Planter. Crown 8vo, cloth. Rs. 3-8.

A Theory of Lunar Surfacing by Glaciation. By S. E. PEAL, Liverpool Astronomical Association. With Illustrations. Royal 8vo. Rs. 2.

Hindu Tribes and Castes. By the Rev. M. A. SHERRING, M.A., LL.B., Lond. In 3 vols. Cloth. Rs. 40.

"Mr. Sherring's work is systematically and clearly arranged. Every caste, from the highest Brahmin to the lowest classes of aborigines and outcasts, is passed in review. . . . This is the first attempt, we believe, to give anything like a general survey of the caste-system as it exists in the Bengal Presidency. Mr. Sherring has well studied his subject, and he writes well and clearly."—*Saturday Review.*

From the City of Palaces to Ultima Thule. With a Map of Iceland, Icelandic Vocabulary, Money Tables, &c. Crown 8vo, sewed. Re. 1.

Splendidly Illustrated book of Sport. In Demy 4to; Rs. 25; elegantly bound. (£2 2s.)

Large Game Shooting in Thibet, the Himalayas, and Northern India. By Colonel ALEXANDER A. KINLOCH. Containing descriptions of the country and of the various animals to be found; together with extracts from a journal of several years' standing. With thirty illustrations and map of the district.

"It is the work of a genuine shikari . . . The heads have been admirably reproduced by the photograph. The spiral or curved horns, the silky hair, the fierce glance, the massive jaws, the thick neck of deer, antelope, yak or bison, are realistic and superior to anything that we can remember in any bookshelf full of Indian sport."—*Saturday Review.*

"The splendidly illustrated record of sport. The photo-gravures, especially the heads of the various antelopes, are lifelike; and the letterpress is very pleasant reading."—*Graphic.*

Musketry Made Easy for Native Officers and Non-Commissioned Officers, Native Army. By Lieutenant R. E. S. TAYLOR, Adjutant, 38th Bengal Infantry. Arranged in Questions and Answers. English and Urdu. Second Edition. As. 8.

The Invasion and Defence of England. By Captain F. N. MAUDE, R.E. Crown 8vo. Re. 1-8.

The Second Bombardment and Capture of Fort William, Calcutta, 20th June, 1891, by a Russian Fleet and Army. Translated from the Russian, by IVAN BATIUSHKA. Crown 8vo. Re. 1-8.

The Quartermaster's Almanac. A Diary of the Duties, with other information. By Lt. H. BUSH. 8vo. Re. 1-8.

The Teeth: their Structure, Disease, and Pre-servation; with some Notes on Conservative and Prosthetic Dentistry. By J. MILLER, L.D.S., R.C.S.E. 9 Plates. Second Edition. Rs. 2-8.

The Indian Medical Service. A Guide for intended Candidates for Commissions and for the Junior Officers of the Service. By W. WILFRED WEBB, M.B., Surgeon, Bengal Army. Crown 8vo. Rs. 4 (5s. 6d.)

Notes on the Course of Garrison Instruction, with diagrams. By Major E. LLOYD, Garrison Instructor. Crown 8vo.

The Indian Articles of War. Annotated. By Captain H. S. HUDSON, 27th Madras Infantry. Crown 8vo. Cloth. Rs. 4.

Hand-Book to the Drill in "Extended Order." Part III. Field Exercise. 1884. With Plates.

Firminger's Manual of Gardening for India. A New Edition, thoroughly Revised and Re-written. With many Illustrations. By J. H. JACKSON, Editor, *Indian Agriculturist*. In the press.

English Etiquette for Indian Gentlemen. By W. TREGO WEBB, Bengal Educational Department. Fcap. 8vo. Re. 1. Cloth, Re. 1-4.

Musketry Instruction in the form of Question and Answer. By Captain L. E. DUMOULIN. Rs. 2.

Letters on Tactics and Organization. The Relationship of British to Continental Systems. By Captain F. N. MAUDE, R.E. Crown 8vo. Rs. 5.

The Captain's Daughter. A Novel literally translated from the Russian. By S: H. GODFREY, Bombay S.C. Rs. 2.
Literally translated, with a view of assisting Students to acquire a Mastery of Russian Idioms, and to obtain a grasp of the Language. This is certainly a very pleasant way of learning Russian.—*Army and Navy Gazette.*

Russian Conversation - Grammar (on the System of Otto). With Exercises, Colloquial Phrases, and an English Russian Vocabulary. By A. KINLOCH, late Interpreter to H.B.M. Consulate, St. Petersburgh. Rs. 6-8 (9s.)
Constructed on the excellent system of Otto, with Illustrations accompanying every rule in the form of usual phrases and idioms; thus leading the Student by easy and rapid gradations to a colloquial knowledge of the Language.

LAW PUBLICATIONS.

The Code of Criminal Procedure: being Act X. of 1882 (amended 1886 and 1887), with Notes of all Judgments and Orders thereon. By H. T. PRINSEP, Judge of the Supreme Court, Calcutta. 8vo. Reprinting.

The Code of Criminal Procedure. Together with Rulings, Circular Orders, Notifications, &c., of all the High Courts in India, and Notifications and Orders of the Government of India and the Local Governments. Edited, with Copious Notes and full Index, by W. F. AGNEW, and GILBERT S. HENDERSON, M.A., Barristers-at-Law. Second Edition. Royal 8vo., cloth. Rs. 18 (36s.)

Al Siràjiyyah: or the Mahommedan Law of Inheritance. Sir William Jones' Translation, with Notes and Appendix by ALMARIC RUMSEY, Professor of Indian Jurisprudence King's College, London. Second Edition. Crown 8vo.

Manual of Revenue and Collectorate Law: with Important Rulings and Annotations. By H. A. D. PHILLIPS, Bengal Civil Service. Crown 8vo. cloth. Rs. 10.

The Negotiable Instruments Act, 1881: being an Act to define and amend the Law relating to Promissory Notes, Bills of Exchange and Cheques. Edited by M. D. CHALMERS, M.A., Barrister-at-Law, Author of "A Digest of the Law of Bills of Exchange," &c., and Editor of Wilson's "Judicature Acts." 8vo., cloth. Rs. 7-8 (10s. 6d.)

The Insolvent Debtors (India) Act. Being a Reprint of Act 11 & 12 Vict., Cap. 21. 8vo. Sewed. Rs. 1-8.

A Commentary on Hindu Law of Inheritance, Succession, Partition, Adoption, Marriage, Stridhan, and Testamentary Disposition. By Pundit JOGENDRO NATH BHATTACHARJI SMARTA SIROMANI, M.A., D.L. Demy 8vo. Cloth, gilt. Rs. 12.

A Chaukidari Manual; being Act VI. (B.C.) of 1870, as amended by Acts 1. (B.C.) of 1871 and 1886. With Notes, Rules, Government Orders, and Inspection Notes. By G. TOYNBEE, C.S., Magistrate of Hooghly. Crown 8vo. cloth. R. 1.

Manual of the Revenue Sale Law and Certificate
Procedure of Lower Bengal, being Act XI. of 1859; Act
VII. (B.C.) of 1868; and Act VII. (B.C.) of 1880: The
Public Demands Recovery Act, including Selections from
the Rules and Circular Orders of the Board of Revenue.
With Notes. By W. H. GRIMLEY, B.A., C.S. 8vo.
Rs. 5-8; interleaved, Rs. 6.

The North-Western Provinces' Rent Act, being
Act XII. of 1881, as amended by Act. XIV. of 1886,
With Notes, &c. By H. W. REYNOLDS, C.S. Demy 8vo.,
cloth. Rs. 7.

The Bengal Tenancy Act. Being Act VIII. of 1885.
With Notes and Annotations, Judicial Rulings, and the
Rules framed by the Local Government and the High Court
under the Act. For the guidance of Revenue Officers and
the Civil Courts. By R. F. RAMPINI, M.A., C.S., Barrister-
at-Law, District and Session Judge, and M. FINUCANE,
M.A., C.S., Director of the Agricultural Department,
Government of Bengal. Second Edition. Royal 8vo. Rs. 7.

The Inland Emigration Act; with Orders by the
Lieutenant-Governor of Bengal; Forms by Government of
Bengal; Resolution of the Government of India; Resolu-
tion of the Government of Assam; Rules made by the
Chief Commissioner of Assam, and Orders by the Lieutenant-
Governor, N. W. P. Interpaged with blank pages for notes.
Crown 8vo. Rs. 2-4.

The Hindu Law of Inheritance, Partition and
Adoption according to the Smritis. By Dr. JULIUS JOLLY,
Tagore Law Lecturer, 1883. Rs. 10.

The Bengal Local Self-Government Act (B.C,
Act III of 1885), and the general Rules framed thereunder,
With Critical and Explanatory Notes, Hints regarding
Procedure, and reference to the Leading Cases on the Law
relating to Local Authorities. To which is added an
Appendix containing the principal Acts referred to, &c.,
&c.; and a Full Index. By F. R. STANLEY COLLIER,
B.C.S., Editor of "The Bengal Municipal Act." Crown
8vo. Second Edition. Rs. 5.

An Income Tax Manual, being Act II. of 1886, The
Rules, Rulings and Precedents, &c., and Notes. By W. H.
GRIMLEY, B.A., C.S., Commissioner of Income Tax, Bengal.
Royal 8vo. Rs. 3-8; interleaved, Rs. 4.

The Pocket Penal, Criminal Procedure and Police
Codes; also the Whipping Act and the Railway Servants' Act. With General Index. Fcap. 8vo., cloth. Rs. 4.

The Pocket Civil Procedure Code, with Court Fee, Indian Evidence, Specific Relief, Indian Registration, Limitation, and Stamp Acts. With General Index. Fcap. 8vo., cloth. Rs. 4.

The Indian Penal Code and other Laws and Acts of Parliament relating to the Criminal Courts of India. With Notes. By J. O'Kinealy, Judge of the High Court, Calcutta. Third Edition. Royal 8vo. Rs. 12 (24s.)

Legislative Acts of the Governor-General of India in Council; published annually with Index. Royal 8vo., cloth. 1872, Rs. 10; 1873, 1874, and 1875, Rs. 5 each; 1876, Rs. 6; 1877, Rs. 10; 1878, Rs. 5; 1879, Rs. 5; 1880, Rs. 4; 1881, Rs. 8; 1882, Rs. 15-8; 1883, Rs. 5; 1884, Rs. 5; 1885, Rs. 5; 1886, Rs. 5; 1887, Rs. 5; 1888, Rs. 5; 1889, Rs.

Introduction to the Regulations of the Bengal Code. By. C. D. Field, M.A., LL.D. (specially reprinted for the use of students, etc.). In crown 8vo., cloth. Rs. 3.

The Law of Evidence in British India. By C. D. Field, M.A., LL.D, Judge of the High Court, Calcutta. Fourth Edition. Rs. 18.

The Indian Contract Act No. IX. of 1872. Together with an Introduction and Explanatory Notes, Table of Contents, Appendix, &c. By H. S. Cunningham, M.A., one of the Judges of H.M.'s High Court of Judicature, Calcutta; and H. H. Shephard, M.A., Barrister-at-Law. Fifth Edition. Rs. 15.

The Practice of the Presidency Court of Small Causes of Calcutta. The Presidency Small Cause Courts Act (XV. of 1882), with Copious Notes; the Code of Civil Procedure, with Notes and References; the Rules of Practice, Institution, and Court Fees; and a complete Index. By R. S. T. MacEwen, Barrister-at-Law, one of the Judges of the Presidency Court of Small Causes of Calcutta. Thick 8vo. Rs. 10.

Introduction to the Duties of Magistrates and Justices of the Peace in India. By Sir P. Benson Maxwell, Kt. Specially edited for India by the Honble. L. P. Delves Broughton, Barrister-at-Law. Royal 8vo. cloth, lettered. Rs. 12.

The Indian Limitation Act; Act XV. of 1877. (As amended by Act XII. of 1879, and subsequent enactments), with Notes. By H. T. RIVAZ, Barrister-at-Law, Advocate, N.-W.-P., and Punjab. Third Edition. Royal 8vo., cloth. Rs. 10.

The Law of Specific Relief in India; being a Commentary on Act I. of 1877. By CHARLES COLLETT, late of the Madras Civil Service, of Lincoln's Inn, Barrister-at-Law, and formerly a Judge of the High Court at Madras. Demy 8vo. Rs. 10 (14s.)

Manual of Indian Criminal Law: being the Penal Code, Criminal Procedure Code, Evidence, Whipping, General Clauses, Police, &c., Acts, with Penal Clauses of Legal Practitioners' Act, Registration, Arms, Stamp, &c., Acts. Fully Annotated, and containing all applicable Rulings of all High Courts arranged under the appropriate Sections up to date. By H. A. D. PHILLIPS. Thick crown 8vo. New Edition. Rs. 10.

Glossary of Medical and Medico-legal Terms, including those most frequently met with in Courts. Compiled by R. F. HUTCHINSON, M.D., Surgeon-Major. Second edition. 18mo., cloth. Rs. 2.

The Stamp Law of British India, as constituted by the Indian Stamp Act (I. of 1879). Rulings and Circular Orders of the four High Courts; Notifications; Resolutions; Rules; and Orders of the Government of India and of the various Local Governments; together with Schedules of all the stamp duties chargeable on Instruments in India from the earliest times. Edited, with Notes and Index, by WALTER R. DONOGH, M.A., of the Inner Temple, Barrister-at-Law. Demy 8vo. Rs. 8.

Code of Civil Procedure (Act XIV. of 1882 as amended by subsequent Acts). With Notes, &c. By J. O'KINEALY, C.S., Judge of the High Court, Calcutta. Fifth Edition. Royal 8vo. Rs. 16.

Law of Intestate and Testamentary Succession in India, including the Indian Succession Act (x. of 1865), with a Commentary, and the Parsee Succession Act, Hindu Wills Act, Probate and Administration Act, District Delegates Act, Acts xii. and xiii. of 1855, Regimental Debts Acts, Acts relating to the Administrator-General Certificate Act, and Oudh Estates Act, with Notes and Cross References and a General Index. By GILBERT S. HENDERSON, M.A., Barrister-at-Law. Rs. 16.

Comparative Criminal Jurisprudence, being a synopsis of the law, procedure, and case law of other countries, arranged as far as possible under the corresponding sections of the Indian Codes. By H. A. D. PHILLIPS.

Vol. I. Crimes and Punishments. Vol. II. Procedure and Police. Rs. 12.

This work includes extracts from the Penal and Criminal Procedure Codes of the State of New York, of Louisiana, of France, Belgium, and Germany, the English statute-law and case-law (up to date), as well as the most important decisions of the Courts of various American States, the Supreme Court of the United States, and the Court of Cassation in Paris; also extracts from the best works on criminal law and jurisprudence.

The Indian Law Examination Manual. By FENDALL CURRIE, Esq., of Lincoln's Inn, Barrister-at-Law. Third Edition. Demy 8vo. Rs. 5.

CONTENTS :—Introduction—Hindoo Law—Mahomedan Law—Indian Penal Code—Code of Civil Procedure—Evidence Act—Limitation Act—Succession Act—Contract—Registration Act—Stamp Acts and Court Fees—Mortgage—Code of Criminal Procedure—The Easement Act—The Trust Act—The Transfer of Property Act—The Negotiable Instruments Act.

The Law of Mortgage in India, including the Transfer of Property, with Notes of Decided Cases. The Second Edition of the Tagore Law Lectures, 1876. Revised and partly rewritten. By RASHBEHARY GHOSE, M.A., D.L. Rs. 10.

The Bengal Municipal Manual, containing the Municipal Act (B. C. Act III. of 1884) and other Laws relating to Municipalities in Bengal, with the Rules and Circulars issued by the Local Government, and Notes. Second Edition, Revised and Enlarged. By F. R. STANLEY COLLIER, B.C.S. Crown 8vo., cloth. Rs. 5.

Possession in the Civil Law, abridged from the Treatise of VON SAVIGNY. To which is added the Text of the *Title* on *Possession* from the *Digest*, with Notes. Compiled by J. KELLEHER, Esq., Bengal Civil Service. Rs. 8.

Principles of Specific Performance and Mistake. By J. KELLEHER, Esq., Bengal Civil Service. Rs. 8.

TAGORE LAW LECTURES.

The Hindu Law; as administered to Hindus by British Courts. (1870 and 1871.) By HERBERT COWELL. Royal 8vo., 2 vols., cloth, each Rs. 8.

History and Constitution of the Courts and Legislative Authorities. (1872.) By HERBERT COWELL. New Edition. (1884). Demy 8vo. Rs. 6.

Mahomedan Law. By SHAMA CHURN SIRCAR.
Digest of Laws according to Sunni Code. Rs. 9. (1873.)
Sunni Code in part and Imamyah Code. Rs. 9. (1874.)

The Law relating to the Land Tenures of Lower Bengal. (1875.) By ARTHUR PHILLIPS. Rs. 10.

The Law relating to Mortgage in India. (1876.) By RASH BEHARI GHOSE. Second Edition. Rs. 10.

The Law relating to Minors in Bengal. (1877.) By E. J. TREVELYAN. Royal 8vo., cloth. Rs. 10.

The Hindu Law of Marriage and Stridhana. (1878.) By GOOROO DOSS BANERJEE. Royal 8vo. Rs. 10.

The Law relating to the Hindu Widow. By TRAILOKYANATH MITTRA, M.A., D.L. Rs. 10. (1879.)

The Principles of the Hindu Law of Inheritance. By RAJCOOMAR SARVADHICARI, B.L. Rs. 16. (1880.)

The Law of Trusts in British India. By W. F. AGNEW, Esq. Rs. 12. (1881).

The Law of Limitation and Prescription in British India. By OPENDRA NATH MITTER. (1882.)

The Hindu Law of Inheritance, Partition, and Adoption, according to the Smritis. By Dr. JULIUS JOLLY. (1883.) Rs. 10.

The Law relating to Gifts, Trusts, and Testa-mentary Dispositions among the Mahomedans. By SYED AMEER ALI. (1884.) Rs. 12.

The Joint Hindu Family in Bengal. By KRISHNA KAMAL BHATTACHERJYA. 1885. Rs. 12.

PUBLISHED IN CALCUTTA ANNUALLY.
Super Royal 8vo.   Leather backs, 36s.

THACKER'S INDIAN DIRECTORY,

Embracing the whole Empire governed by the Viceroy of India and also the Native States; with complete and detailed information of the Cities of Calcutta, Bombay and Madras. With Almanac, Army List, and general information.

"Nothing more strikingly represents the change that has come over India in recent years than this great Directory. Here is seen at a glance the vast development of our industries, the growth of the white population, the increased pressure of competition, and all the manifold interests which go to make up the complex fabric of Anglo-Indian life in these days."—*Englishman,* Calcutta.

"The alphabetical list of residents throughout India in the three great provinces, with their addresses, must be of great service to those who have business with our Eastern Empire."—*The Times* (London).

"Aims at being a directory to the whole of India. It contains separate classified and street directories of each of the cities of Calcutta, Bombay, and Madras, a remarkably comprehensive and detailed Mofussil directory, and a vast amount of general information relating to India, its government, commerce, postal arrangements, festivals, and official establishments. . . The expansion of the work will be welcomed as a response to the growing requirements of commerce with India."—*Manchester Guardian.*

Published Monthly.   Subscriptions Rs. 18 *per Annum, including Postage.*

THE INDIAN MEDICAL GAZETTE.

A Record of Medicine, Surgery, and Public Health, and of General Medical Intelligence, Indian and European. Edited by K. McLeod, M.D.

The Indian Medical Gazette has for more than twenty years earned for itself a growing and world-wide reputation by its solid contributions to Tropical Medicine and Surgery. It is the sole representative medium for recording the work and experience of the Medical Profession in India; and its arrangements with the leading Medical Journals in Great Britain and America enable it not only to diffuse this information broadcast throughout the world, but also to cull for its Indian readers, from an unusual variety of sources, all information which has any practical bearing on medical works in India.

The Contributors to *The Indian Medical Gazette* comprise the most eminent and representative men in the profession, and the contents form a storehouse of information on tropical diseases which would otherwise be lost to the world.

INDEX TO GENERAL PUBLICATIONS.

	PAGE
Ali, Critical Exposition of "Jihad"	16
Amateur Gardener in the Hills	9
Anderson, Mandalay to Momien	16
Baillie, Kurrachee	5
Barker, Tea Planter's Life in Assam	10
Batiushka, Bombardment of Calcutta	20
Beddome, Ferns of India, Ceylon, &c.	3
Behind the Bungalow	2
Bell, Laws of Wealth	19
Beveridge, Emperor Akbar	8
Beveridge, Trial of Nanda Kumar	19
Bignold, Leviora	12
Birch, Management of Children in India	10
Bonavia, Date Palm in India	16
Bose, The Hindoos as they are	13
Boutflower, Statics and Dynamics	18
Busteed, Echoes from old Calcutta	9
C——, Major, Indian Horse Notes	9
C——, Major, Indian Notes about Dogs	8
Cæsar de Souza	12
Calcutta Turf Club Calendar	12
Calcutta Turf Club Rules	12
Coldstream, Grasses of the Punjab	11
Ceylon Tea Estates	10
City of Palaces to Ultima Thule	20
Captain's Daughter, from the Russian, by Godfrey	21
Cunningham, Indian Eras	17
Duke, Banting in India	14
Duke, Queries at a Mess Table	15
Dutt, Civilization in Ancient India	12
Field, Landholding	15
Firminger, Gardening for India	21
Fletcher, Poppied Sleep	17
Forbes, British Burma	16
Fauna of British India	11
Government of India, Primer	12
Gregg, Text-Book of Indian Botany	15
Harrington, Ashes for Bread	15
Harris, Bengal Medical Service	17
Hayes, Riding on the Flat and Across Country	6
Hayes, Veterinary Notes for Horse Owners	6
Hayes, Points of the Horse	6
Hayes, The Horsewoman	6
Hayes, Sporting News	6

INDEX TO GENERAL PUBLICATIONS—*continued*.

	PAGE
Hayes, Indian Racing Reminiscences ...	8
Hayes, Training and Horse Management	7
Hayes, On Tactics	7
Hayes, Soundness in Horses	7
Hayes, Illustrated Horse Breaking	7
Humfrey, Horse Breeding in India	9
Ince, Guide to Kashmir	18
India in 1983	12
Indian Tea Gardens, &c., A Complete List	10
Jackson, Statistics of Hydraulic Works, &c.	13
Keene, Handbook to Agra	18
Keene, Handbook to Allahabad	18
Keene, Handbook to Delhi	18
Keshub Chunder Sen, Life and Teaching	9
Kinloch, Large Game Shooting...	20
Kinloch, Russian Conversation-Grammar	21
Kipling, Departmental Ditties...	4
Kipling, Plain Tales from the Hills	8
Kuropatkin, (Gowan) Kashgaria	16
Lays of Ind, by Aliph Cheem ...	4
Le Messurier, Game, Shore and Water Birds of India	13
Lyon, Medical Jurisprudence for India	8
Map of Civil Divisions of India	17
Maude's Invasion and Defence of England	20
McCrindle, Ancient India	17
Meerza, Mohammadan Social Reform	14
Military Hand Book, Drill in Extended Order	21
„ Articles of War ... ... Hudson	21
„ Musketry Instruction... ... Dumoulin	21
„ Musketry Made Easy ... Taylor	20
„ Sepoy Officers' Manual ... Barrow	19
„ Reconnoitrer's Guide ... King-Harman...	11
„ Tactics and Organization ... Maude	21
„ On Garrison Instruction ... Lloyd ...	21
Miller, The Teeth	21
Mookerjee, Memoir of Onoocool Chunder Mookerjee	13
Murray-Aynsley, Hills beyond Simla ...	18
Norman, Calcutta to Liverpool...	18
Northam, Guide to Masuri, &c...	18
O'Connell, Ague ...	17
O'Donoghue, Riding for Ladies	3
Peal, Lunar Surfacing by Glaciation ...	19
Phillips, Our Administration of India...	11
Pogson, Agriculture for India ...	16

INDEX TO GENERAL PUBLICATIONS—*continued.*

	PAGE
Pollard, Indian Tribute and the Loss by Exchange	19
Pollard, Gold and Silver weighed in the Balance	19
Pool, Queen Victoria	17
Protestant Missions	17
Quartermaster's Almanac	21
Ranking, Guide to Hindustani	14
Ranking, Hidyat al Hukuma	14
Reid, Indigo Culture and Manufacture	12
Reminiscences of Behar	19
Richards, Landmarks of Snake Poison Literature	17
Romance of Thakote	15
Rowe, Key to Entrance Course, 1888	19
Rowe and Webb, Hints on the Study of English	14
Rowe and Webb, Companion Reader to the Study of English	14
Roxburgh's Flora Indica	16
Sedgwick, Life	18
Sherring, Hindu Tribes and Castes	20
Sherring, Light and Shade	15
Son Gruel	18
Sterndale, Mammalia of India	5
Sterndale, Denizens of the Jungles	5
Sterndale, Seonee	19
Sterndale, Calcutta Collectorate	18
Tagore, Bombay Sketches	12
Thacker's Guide to Calcutta	18
Thacker's Indian Directory	28
Thuillier, Manual of Surveying for India	13
Tribes on my Frontier	2
Tsaya (Powell) Myam-Ma	16
Tweedie, Hindustani as Spoken	14
Underwood, Indian-English and Indian Character	19
Useful Hints to Young Shikaris	5
Walker, Fishing in Kumaun Lakes	14
Webb, Indian Medical Service	21
Webb, Key to Entrance Course	19
Webb, English Etiquette for Indian Gentlemen	21
Webb, Indian Lyrics	14
Wheeler, Tales from Indian History	12
Wilkins, Hindu Mythology	8
Wilkins, Modern Hinduism	19
Wood, Fifty Graduated Papers in Arithmetic, &c.	14
Wyvern, Culinary Jottings	15
Wyvern, Sweet Dishes	15

INDEX TO LAW BOOKS.

		PAGE
Al Sirájiyyah (Mahommedan Inheritance) ...	Rumsey ...	22
Bengal Code, Introduction to Regulations ...	Field	24
Bengal Local Self-Government	Collier	23
Bengal Tenancy Act	Rampini and Finucane ...	23
Criminal Jurisprudence, Comparative... ...	Phillips... ...	26
Criminal Law	do.	25
Criminal Procedure	Prinsep... ...	22
Criminal Procedure	Agnew and Henderson	22
Civil Procedure, Evidence, &c. ("The Pocket")	... ...	24
Civil Procedure	O'Kinealy ...	25
Contract Act	Cunningham and Shephard	24
Contract Act	Macrae ...	22
Courts and Legislative Authorities	Cowell	27
Chaukidari Manual	Toynbee ...	22
Emigration Act, Inland...	... ...	23
Evidence, Law in British India	Field	24
Examination Manual	Currie	26
Gifts, Trusts and Testamentary, Mahomedan ...	Ameer Ali ...	27
Hindu Law	Cowell	27
Hindu Widows	Mittra	27
Income Tax Manual	Grimley ...	23
Inheritance, &c., Hindu	Siromani ...	22
Inheritance, &c. ,, ...	Jolly	23
Inheritance, &c. ,, ...	Sarvadhicari ...	27
Insolvent Debtors Act	... ...	22
Land Tenures, Bengal	Phillips ...	27
Law Examination Manual	Currie ...	26
Legislative Acts	"Annual" ...	24
Limitation and Prescription	Mitter	27
Limitation	Rivaz	25
Magistrates, Duties of	Maxwell ...	24
Medical and Medico-legal Terms	Hutchinson ...	25
Municipal Act, Bengal	Collier	26
Mahomedan Law	Sircar	27
Minors	Trevelyan ...	27
Marriage and Stridhana	Banerjee ...	27
Mortgage	Ghose	26
Negotiable Instruments...	Chalmers ...	22
Penal Code ("The Pocket")	... ...	24
Penal Code	O'Kinealy ...	24
Possession in the Civil Law	Kelleher ...	26
Rent Act (N.W.P.)	Reynolds ...	23
Revenue and Collectorate Law	Phillips... ...	22
Revenue Sale and Certificate	Grimley ...	23
Stamp Law	Donogh... ...	25
Small Cause Court Act, Presidency	McEwen ...	24
Specific Relief	Collett	25
Specific Performance and Mistake	Kelleher ...	26
Succession, Intestate and Testamentary ...	Henderson ...	25
Trusts	Agnew... ..	27
Tagore Law Lectures	Various ...	27

www.ingramcontent.com/pod-product-compliance
Lightning Source LLC
Chambersburg PA
CBHW031932230426
43672CB00010B/1903